Seacat Simon

The little cat who became a big hero

by

Jacky Donovan

Simon's tale is based on a true story. Apart from the following people, all names in this book are fictitious and any resemblance to real persons, living or dead, is purely coincidental.

Lieutenant Commander Ian Griffiths
Lieutenant Commander K. Stewart Hett
Lieutenant Commander John S. Kerans
Lieutenant Commander Bernard Skinner
First Lieutenant Geoffrey L. Weston

CONTENTS

Prologue

I'm curled up, all snuggly and warm beside George, just ready for a nice little snooze. I can feel the ship's engine thudding, thudding. I can hear it too, really hear it. It gets louder and louder until suddenly — bang! I'm thrown right off the bed and onto the floor.

All the sailors must hear it too because they spring out of their beds. What *is* this? I dash out onto the deck and run up to the bow. Huge things are whizzing over my head and hitting the ship. I scamper off to try and escape them.

'I do believe someone's firing at us.' The Captain looks and sounds surprised. 'Action stations,' he snaps and some of the men leap over me and rush away. A horrible sound runs all around the ship, making my whole body shake and hurting my ears, my head. Make it stop!

Another huge bang and crash and I'm thrown right across the floor. I try to stand up, but I can't. Even though I can put my front paws onto the floor, my back legs won't move. Everything underneath me has tilted and there is thick, black smoke coming in from outside. It gets up my nose and makes my eyes sting. There's a loud noise between my ears. I shake my head and try to stand. It's getting darker, hotter.

There's a nasty, burning smell too. I can't see or hear. It's hard to even breathe. My whiskers, my ears, my fur, everything's standing on end. What's happening?

Painfully, I lift myself up and slowly manage to crawl through the doorway. I try to get away from the noise, but it's even louder outside. Another bang, a thud and the ship tilts again. As I watch the men unfold a large sheet, there's another bang and two of the men fall down.

The sheet the men unroll is a flag. They hang it over the side of the ship. Even though I know what a flag is, I don't know why they're doing it now. It seems a strange time to unroll a flag just to show where you're from.

1

Maybe I should hide until the noise stops and the smoke and the banging go away. But where?

No, I want to be brave, need to be brave! Slowly, I crawl up to the bow and look out. Thick, dirty smoke hangs above the water. I look out across it and try to see through it.

The smoke clears a bit over the water and I think I can make out a dark shape. I keep on looking to try and work out what it is. It's a ship, smaller than this one, with lots of men on it. So why are they doing this if they're the same as us?

At that moment, amongst the men, I spot another shape, something small and fuzzy. It's moving around between their legs. It glances up and I spy one glinting green eye staring right back at me. Oh no! It can't be, can it...?

Another bang explodes in my ears, making them scream again. My legs hurt, my ears hurt, all of me hurts. I think I see Peggy and I try to make some kind of sound, but I can't. My head's heavy. It drops and I fall sideways onto the deck. The brightness turns to black, the screaming replaced...

By silence.

1/ Friends are fun

One year earlier

I feel some claws digging into my back and I turn around. It's Uboat, my friend. He appears sometimes then disappears and comes back again. He likes to jump on board the ships that come into the harbour and go away on them.

I smile when I see him and my whiskers twitch. They always do that when I'm happy. We rub noses. He smells of salty water and his fur's sticky.

'Where've you been?'

'Where haven't I been?' He half laughs, half purrs and jumps onto my back. 'I've been watching the seagulls on the sea and running up and down on a big boat. It's been fun, fun, fun!'

'And what else? What else have you seen?' I like Uboat's adventures. He's told me about places where everyone and everything belongs to a king. Of Captains on ships, whales in the sea and dogs on the land. About tigers which are like big "me"s and creatures called monkeys. Whales, dogs, tigers, monkeys… I wonder what sort of creature me and Uboat are? All I know is I am me, so I must be a "me", and Uboat must be a "me" like me too!

'This time I've seen green birds that talk to you. I've played on lots of sand next to the sea and burnt my paws. Once, when the ship landed somewhere, I jumped off and got chased by lots of children. They said they'd never seen anything like me before. They just wanted to play and give me *lots* of nice food. It was fun, fun, fun!'

Uboat rolls on his back and waves his legs in the air before jumping to his feet again. 'And what about you, what have you been doing?' he asks

'I've been playing in the alley and running in between legs and watching the birds,' I say, sitting up and licking a paw.

'Always watching, aren't you? Watching, watching. Have you ever woken up and not known where you are?'

'No. I *always* know where I am.'

'I know you do,' Uboat laughs. 'But can you remember what this place is even called?'

'Of course I can,' I say, trying to remember. I know Uboat told me once. 'It's called Ding Dong.'

Uboat lets out another loud laugh. 'Ha, ha. It's called Hong Kong, not Ding Dong. And this part is called Stonecutters Island.'

I feel very silly, but pretend not to be.

'Well, what does it matter what places are called as long as you like living where you are?'

'I don't know. It seems to matter to humans though.'

'Why?'

'Because if you know where you're from then you also know where you're not from. They like to know these things,' he continues, nodding at three pairs of human legs as they rush past us.

'But why?'

'Because then you can protect the place where you're from.'

'Protect it from what?' I ask, confused.

'Others who aren't from there, I suppose.' Uboat answers.

From. Not from. Now my head's spinning. What's wrong with wanting to go to a place and play in it if it's nice? Uboat isn't from here, but that doesn't mean I don't like it when he jumps off his ship and comes to find me.

'I like watching the birds flying high, high, high and swooping low above the port,' I tell him. 'I wish I could fly away.'

The blast of a horn makes me twitch and blink away the picture of me flying. How funny.

'I'd like to fly just for a little bit to see what it was like, but not all the time. I like my paws. And I wouldn't want to fly away forever.'

'You could fly, fly fly, and have fun, fun, fun,' Uboat laughs. 'You won't stay here forever, I bet.' He bats at a bird as it swoops low, but it swooshes off.

'I know this is the one life I have and the one life I want,' I tell him. 'It's *my* life and I know this is where I want to be. I don't want to be anywhere else. Why would I?'

4

There's the port for one thing, full of huge ships coming in from the big sea and others going away. Some have funnels on them and many of them have sheets tied to the mast. Although I can't make out all the different colours, I know the sheets are really called flags. The flags on the ships mean the ships come from places all over the world. They sail in from the big sea that connects all the places up.

'You could sail away with me,' Uboat swipes at me with a paw.

'I like being with JoJo too much,' I mew. JoJo's my big brother. I love having a big brother. He has black fur like me, but I have white paws as well and my tail is longer. Once we had a mother too. That's where we came from. I see pictures of her sometimes in my head, but I don't remember her. I'm happy I'm here now, with JoJo, and we have each other. I don't know what I'd do without him.

'I like seeing the fish, though,' I tell Uboat as he puts his paw into the water's edge and tries to catch a fish.

'Come on, let's catch one,' Uboat grins.

'Noooo,' I mew. 'I don't like to get my paws or my ears or my tail wet. Not if I can help it. No thank you!'

Uboat laughs when I tell him that. But I don't want to stop the little fish from being able to swim. I like seeing them, all happy to be free.

I like to sit here. Or lie down. In the sun, stretch my legs out. Feel the heat warm my fur even more as I lie on my back and just... streeetch.

2/ Coming and going

The birds are flying high, high, high and swooping low above the port. When it gets hot, a lot of the birds will fly away from the harbour.

I wish I could fly away.

The blast of a horn makes me twitch and blink away the picture of me flying. I like it here too much to want to fly away forever.

Sometimes, JoJo might want to show me somewhere new he's found. So we trot along the harbour, jump up the steps — two, four, five — turn into the alley and scamper away from the port. Passing vegetable stalls and stopped chickens on bamboo poles, running in and out between all the legs of the humans, my head swims with all the different smells that tickle my nose. Fishy then meaty then smoky.

I want to stop and investigate, but instead I run, run, run, rushing past men and women, wheels of carts, black cars, everything and everyone hurrying, shouting. Busy, busy, fast, fast.

We'll get to where he wants us to be and what he wants to show me. A new, quiet place to play or hide, or where lots of legs sit down and eat. The smell makes me very hungry. Sometimes an owner sees us and throws us some food. Once or twice we get chased out. My tail's been caught under a broom before now and, when it happens, I yelp and have to run even faster.

Every so often, near the sloping grass, children run around and play with a ball. Sometimes JoJo runs over and tries to chase it. And sometimes, when we have a ball to play with, he finds a box, tips it to one side and I have to stop him from getting the ball into the box. He's *very* clever. But often when I want to just lie in the box, JoJo pushes it over on me so I can't get out. He's not very nice sometimes too!

Whenever we come down the hill and it's getting to dark time, we pass a building with men and women going in. The smell of the women is nicer than the smell at the top of the grassy slope. It makes my nose twitch and sometimes I even sneeze. They look very pink and pretty and they smile at me a lot.

They're always with men who look very stiff in their uniforms, but their buttons glint and shine and sometimes they smile at me too. Whenever lovely sounds come from inside there are always men and women moving around close together and it makes me want to wiggle my bottom a little bit.

We don't play round there very often though. There's a mean grey me with one green eye who hisses and chases us away whenever we see him. He's called Chairman and he's *horrible*. Even JoJo's scared of him. The last time we saw Chairman he came right up close to us and spat, 'This place is mine. I live here. If I ever see you here again then a *very bad thing* will happen to you…' I don't know why he doesn't like us when we could all play together, but JoJo says he's nasty which means he's very bad and naughty.

Not every me who lives round here is horrible though. Sometimes I see a very pretty me called Lilette running around and playing. She's all white, has one big blue and one big gold eye and I like her a *lot*. We don't play together though. I just see her and smile and she smiles back. JoJo tells me I shouldn't be so shy and just say hello. I did say hello to her once, but she didn't say anything which made me feel very small and silly so I just gave up.

So yes, I like it here because of all those things. Apart from Chairman and some of the humans that chase me sometimes, I know there's more good than bad.

3/ King of the land

I look at Uboat.

'So, how long are you in this place for?' I ask him. 'On Stormcutters Island?'

'Stonecutters not Stormcutters,' Uboat laughs. 'I heard the men on the ship say we're here to collect some stores and then we'll be going again.'

'Where are you going to this time?' I want to know.

'Who knows? Who knows?' Uboat pounces onto my tail. 'Somewhere with lots of exciting new smells and places to explore.'

'Don't you ever get scared you might get wet when you're on a ship?' My left ear twitches.

'I do get wet sometimes,' he laughs. 'But it's all part of the fun. You get used to it.'

A quick shiver runs through my little body at the very thought and all the way down to my tail that Uboat's now playfully pulling with his teeth.

'Let's run.'

'Where to?' I ask him. It's still hot on my fur and I want to carry on lying here and look at the boats and the ships, at the birds and at all the humans hurrying around. They might even give me something to eat.

'Wherever our paws take us,' he chuckles and dashes off, through the port and up some steps. 'Come on, come on, come on!'

And so I follow him. He points out his ship, blue and white and huge. We run up steps, past some baskets, in between lots of pairs of legs and into the alley. It's cooler here and a little bit darker.

There are chickens in baskets all piled high. Some of them are talking. Some of them are sitting down. Some have their backs to the door of the cage. All of them look unhappy.

'Poor chickens,' I say to Uboat.

'Yes,' he twitches his nose. 'They'll never know what it's like to be free, free, free on the open sea, sea, sea.' He looks sad. 'They do taste nice though.' And then he laughs.

'Uboat!' I don't like the thought of things moving around and then *stopping*. Even though they do taste nice.

We scamper round the corner and go down a maze of narrow alleyways, twisting and turning. There are yummy smells coming from all around and steam from the pots and from the doorways.

'Uboat,' I call to him and he stops and turns round.

'Yes?' He comes running back to me.

'I'm hungry.'

'So, what shall we do? Where shall we go?' He sniffles a little.

'Maybe if we just stay here they'll throw us some food,' I reply, looking over at one of the women sitting on her doorstep.

She looks over at us both and hisses, 'Shweh, shweh.' She grabs a broom.

'I don't think so,' Uboat responds. 'She has a big, red, angry face. Look.'

I do and he's right.

Suddenly, a grey me comes running towards us. A green eye catches the sun and it glints. It's big, bad, scary Chairman. My back legs wobble, my ears go flat and I have to sit down.

He comes right up to us both and spits and hisses. 'What have I said? What have I said?' he hisses at us. '*I* live here. This is *my* place. Go away!' Uboat squares up to him. His back is arched and his tail is standing straight out.

'And what happens if we *don't* go away?' Uboat has made himself look *very* mean and he sounds different. 'Do you know who I am?'

Chairman looks at him. 'No. I've never seen you before.'

They begin to circle around each other slowly.

'I'm the king of where I'm from,' Uboat snarls. 'I'm looking for a new place to live. And if I decide to live here I'll bring hundreds and hundreds of my kind with me and *you* will be our first prisoner. Our first enemy.'

I don't really understand what Uboat's saying, but it all sounds a bit scary.

Chairman gives another little hiss, but eventually he turns around and slinks off.

'That was *very* brave of you,' I say to Uboat as we laugh together. 'Pretending you were a king.'

We run back to the port, darting through alleyways and running around and over boxes. We get back to one of my best hiding places, right at the end of the harbour. Uboat and I cuddle up together.

'I have to go soon,' Uboat nuzzles me.

I mew sadly.

'Come with me!' he says.

I shake my head. 'I like it here. There's JoJo and there's— '

'Food?' Uboat laughs. 'There's food in other places. Lots of it.'

'No. I like listening to your adventures, but I don't think I'm ready to have an adventure of my own just yet. I'm not big enough.'

'When's big enough?' Uboat smiles, his whiskers twitching. We close our eyes and in my head I see birds flying in the sky and JoJo playing with a big fish and I see my mother. Not that I remember her. She's pretend. But in my head she's big and black and white and warm. It makes me feel nice and I think I purr.

A deep blast of a ship's horn makes me jump.

'I know that sound.' Uboat glances at me. 'I have to go.'

He stands up, puts his front legs forwards and stretches them. His tail swishes past my nose, tickling me.

'Until next time. Enjoy all your fish.'

And he scampers off into the dark. I know I'll see him again though. I always do.

I don't know whether to move or to stay here. I think I may go and find some more food in a bit. For the moment, I'll stay curled up. Under here. Uboat can have his adventures. Watching the humans coming and going is adventure enough for me.

4/ From bad to good

I close my eyes and in my head my mother appears again. She's smiling, smiling. She licks my nose, her big eyes right up close to mine. I'm surrounded by her black and white fur, but suddenly I sniff something. It changes from a smell I think I know to one I don't. I twitch my nose and open my eyes.

I can see a shape moving slowly towards me. I hear a whimper, almost as if it's coming from far away and I recognise it immediately.

'JoJo,' I call out and sit up. The shape twitches and slows down. I run over. It *is* him.

'JoJo, JoJo,' I cry out, nudging his face, nibbling his ear. His other ear is ragged and sticky. He's sticky all over. 'What's happened? What's happened?'

JoJo looks up at me. He can barely move. One of his back legs is twisted. I lick his face, but he closes his eyes.

'You've been playing in the alley with Uboat, haven't you?' He coughs.

'Yes.'

'I smelt you. Then I went looking for you.' He opens his eyes. 'Chairman.'

'Chairman did this?'

'Yes. He jumped on me and scratched me everywhere. He attacked me all the way down the hill.'

'Oh, JoJo, JoJo,' I squeal.

'He said this is for your friend the king… '

I close my eyes when JoJo says that.

'It hurts,' he whimpers.

'Where?' I rub his nose again.

'Everywhere. I have to… You need to— '

And then JoJo closes his eyes again. And he stops.

This does not make sense. This does *not* make sense. I push him with my nose. I lick his face. I even jump on his back and dig my claws in. But it's no use. He's stopped, he's stopped, he's stopped.

I stand up and let out a huge 'Meowww!' And another and another. Somewhere a human shouts. I arch my back. My tail's sticking straight out, all stiff. I jump up and dash behind a box and out again. JoJo's still lying there, stopped.

I don't know what to do, so I run. I run and run and run, through the port, round a corner, turn around and back again. I run behind a box before poking my head out and looking around. I can see the ship Uboat's on edging out of the harbour. Uboat going. JoJo stopped. There are many lights everywhere, twinkling. Why are they twinkling? What is there to light up now?

I cough and cough and a little ball of my dark fur comes up. And then I curl up and screech and shake. I'm all alone. No one is here to protect me. I feel so cold. What shall I do now? Where shall I go?

I crouch behind the box and try to think of a picture, something that might make me jump up and run, to feel warm, to feel nice. But nothing comes. I have nowhere to run and no one to run to.

My tail's sticking straight out behind me again, all stiff. I try to curl it around me, but it won't move. I stretch my front paws, I twitch my ears, but I can't move my tail. I'm frozen. I can't move. What's happening to me?

I close my eyes. Maybe when I open them I won't be here? Maybe when I open them I'll see JoJo?

I hear a noise behind me. I'm too scared to move. There's something behind me. Chairman. He's here. He's found me. He's going to make me stop too. This is it.

I feel my tail being pulled. I'm too scared to make a sound. I stretch my claws out in front of me to try to grab onto the ground, but it's no use.

Oh, I'm being squeezed, but only a little. I open my eyes and turn my head. A human's looking at me. He's smiling and his eyes are a little wet and then I feel his hands are warm.

'Hello, little fella,' he says to me. 'I thought there was something hiding. Your tail was sticking out. Come here, you're shaking.' And he lifts me up and puts me in his arms. Who is he? What's he going to do to me?

He makes me feel all nice and warm. He tries to put me on the ground, but I quite like being in his arms. He must be able to tell I don't want him to let me go because he stands up again and gives me another squeeze. I like being snuggled against his thick coat, all warm. This must be what having a mother is like.

'There, there,' he says. 'D'you want to come with me?'

Maybe I should struggle? Then he would put me down and I could run away. But where would I go? Who would I run to now? I feel safe.

'You sure you don't want me to let you go?'

I bury my head into his arm.

'OK,' he says. 'That settles it,' and before I know it we're walking away from the place where I live and where I'm from, away from the alley, right round the harbour. He's walking so quickly and I feel so high up off the ground I feel like I'm flying, like the birds up in the bright, bright sky. I'm flying, flying, away, away...

5/ A new home

I peek through a gap between the man's coat and his arm and see a huge ship. He stops and looks up. There's something with rails on either side resting on the dock, leading upwards. It looks like a big tongue ready to lick us both up. We step onto it and walk up, wobbling a bit until we get onto the ship.

'Don't make a sound now,' he whispers to me. He doesn't need to tell me to be quiet. I'm shaking too much to make any sort of sound. I peep out from under his arm. I spy some men near the top of the tongue and I shrink right back.

We must creep past them because I can feel him moving and then hear him say, 'OK,' and he taps me on my head through his coat. I peep out, just a little bit. It smells funny. The ship has a different smell to anything I've smelt before.

Even though I've never been on a ship, Uboat says they're fun. It doesn't really feel much like fun right now, but it doesn't feel too scary either. It seems like this man wants to look after me. I blink slowly. I'd rather be close to this strange man than be anywhere near horrible Chairman.

We duck under a chain and underneath some stairs. We go through an open door and step inside the ship itself. It's hotter now and it smells of humans even more. We get underneath what looks like a hiding place. He grabs a big fishing net hanging from a hook, attaches it to another hook and clambers inside. It swings from side to side as we get in. He gets a blanket, puts it over himself and sits me on top of it.

I look at him properly now and he looks right back at me. He smiles again. 'My name's George. I wonder what we shall call you.' His eyebrows move close together. 'I think I'll call you Simon. D'you like being on a ship, Simon?'

Simon?! I ask myself. Simon?! JoJo used to call me Titch. I mew and my whiskers droop. Thinking about JoJo makes me sad.

Perhaps being called Simon will make my whiskers twitch and make me want to run around again? I hope so.

I look around. I'm still trying to get used to all the funny smells. I can see now there are lots of other men in this place too. Like George, they're lying back and swinging in tiny beds hanging up. Some of them are making snuffling, growling noises. It's quite dark, but it means I can see more — a table and some chairs, and pipes running across the roof and lots of other things I don't recognise. I wonder if this is like the inside of the ships Uboat has lived on.

George sits up to take his boots and trousers off. He wraps his boots in his trousers, puts them behind his head and lies back again. I'm not quite sure what to do. I feel a little bit scared, a little bit sad, but a little bit something else as well. Something tells me the best thing for me to do is just to stay here with George so I move round and round ready to settle on him.

I look at his feet. They're *very* dirty and smelly. George makes a little noise, lifts me up and turns me round so I'm facing him.

'Sorry, Simon,' he smiles. 'Your tail was tickling my nose.'

And that reminds me of Uboat again, just before he ran off and left me. I make a promise to myself — and to JoJo: I will *really* try to be brave from now on. Just like Uboat is and JoJo was. Uboat said living on ships and going to different places is fun, but I think he says those things because he doesn't get scared like me. So, I'll try to be like him. To be like both of them.

George's eyes are starting to close, but I want to be awake more than I want to go to sleep. I listen to the other men making noises. George starts to make them too. He seems to be talking in between his snuffles. How funny. I wonder who he's talking to and if he has pictures in his head like I do.

As I close my eyes, I hear another noise. It's a 'clack, clack' sound and I can hear some panting too. My eyes dart around, my ears flatten right back and my whiskers go all quivery. I can smell something as well. Suddenly, a large, furry head appears in the hiding place and stares right at me. Oh no! It's the head of a dog.

6/ Now is all we have

I don't know what to do. I want JoJo! Some of the dogs that run around the harbour want to chase me and eat me up, but some of the others are quite friendly. I wonder if this one's a friend or… not a friend.

I think of JoJo and Uboat being brave so I decide to do that. Or at least pretend. The dog keeps on looking at me. But it hasn't growled or shown me its teeth.

I give a little cough. 'You're a dog,' I say to the furry head, finally.

'Yes, I am,' the dog answers. 'Seadog Peggy at your service.' And she licks my face. 'Who are *you*?'

'I think I'm called Simon,' I reply.

'You only *think* you're called Simon? How frightfully queer,' Peggy replies. 'What are you doing on here?'

'I'm not sure. I was with my brother, and then I was hiding and then… ' I start to whimper.

Peggy puts her wet nose right up to my face. I shift back a little.

'Don't worry,' she mutters. 'I won't bite you. Not all dogs are grumpy, you know.'

Funny how this dog seems to be good yet Chairman, another me, is not.

'Shall I show you around?' she asks.

'I think I'd like that very much. But I think George here wants me to stay put.'

'You think an awful lot,' Peggy snorts. 'I'm more of a, how you would say, a doer myself. I'll bet George here is asleep judging by his snoring, so I vote we go.'

Snoring. What a funny word.

I stand up, which makes the bed wobble and swing even more, and spring onto the floor.

'This way,' says Peggy and I can feel her hot breath on me. It smells even worse than the smell of feet in here. She heads off and I follow her. She has a brown head, a brown and white body and a brown tail. Her bottom wobbles as she pads off. In fact she's quite wobbly all over. She must eat a *lot* of food on this ship. Maybe it won't be so bad after all.

'Is it always so hot here?' I ask her bottom.

'Oh yes,' she replies. 'Except when we're out at sea. Sometimes it's even hotter. You get used to it though.'

As Peggy squeezes through the gap underneath the stairs and I rush through, I notice both Peggy's paws and mine are making that 'clack, clack' sound. We're back outside on the ship's deck. The twinkling stars and the cool breeze are quite nice though, so I decide to lick myself and give myself a quick clean. Peggy barks, making me spring right to my feet and almost fall over.

'Don't jump over the gunwale,' Peggy gives a little laugh.

'What's a gunwale?'

'The sides of the ship. If you go overboard, I'd have to jump over too and fish you out and I'd really rather not do that, thank you very much.' Peggy's tail droops a little.

'Don't you like water?' I ask.

'Gosh, I love water. It's just that I've had a most wonderful brush this evening. Haven't you noticed my frightfully glossy coat?'

Peggy trots off again. 'Come on. Let me take you to the bow.'

She sets off, panting a little and so I follow; little round windows to my left, the — what I now know to be the gunwale — and the sea below to my right. There are many things to jump over, under and through. Such fun! With my whiskers I can judge the gaps and do it very easily, but Peggy has to push herself through. The gaps are not very small really, but I suppose it's harder if you're big.

Although Peggy starts to trot off ahead of me, I catch up with her easily. I can't get past her though and so my head ends right up close to her tail and bottom. As she tries to squeeze through a gap, struggling under the strain, she lifts up her tail and gives a little parp. The smell is even worse than the one from the feet of all the sleeping men in that room!

Peggy turns round. 'I do apologise,' she whispers. 'I do that sometimes.'

My nose wrinkles. What a pong!

Peggy coughs. 'This side of the ship is called the starboard side,' she explains. 'And those boats up there are lifeboats.'

Are boats alive? I didn't think they were.

'And those rings there,' she nods. 'Well, if the men throw them into the water or drop the boats in, it means… well it means an awfully terrible thing has happened probably.'

'What do the rings do?' I ask, puzzled.

'They rescue people,' she answers. 'It means they save lives.'

Just like George saved mine, I think.

We reach some more stairs and start to climb up them. 'And the other side of the ship is called the port,' Peggy continues.

She huffs and puffs as we climb up the steep stairs. I jump from step to step and get to the top much faster than she does. Finally she reaches me. 'And this is called the gun deck.'

So many new words. Uboat never said about any of these things when he was telling me his stories. I look around.

'What are those two long noses?' I ask Peggy.

'Those are called turrets.' She goes up to them and gives them a little sniff. 'They're used to shoot things. They make a terribly deafening sound.'

I give them a little sniff too. 'What does 'shoot' mean?' I ask her. I shoot past things when I run, but I know I don't make a deafening noise.

'So many questions, Simon. Hopefully you'll never need to know what shoot means. Come on.'

We run across the gun deck and get to the very front of the ship. I'm near the tongue again.

'This is the bow,' Peggy says proudly yet panting. I look out. I can see another huge ship just in front and the harbour stretching out to the big sea, all lit up by stars and the lights of the buildings. I try to picture me going out to sea, the cool wind pushing my ears back and with all sorts of birds flying overhead.

21

I turn around. 'What's that?'

'That's the bridge,' Peggy explains, looking all serious now, just like when JoJo tells me — used to tell me — not to gobble up too much food.

'That's not a bridge,' I laugh. 'I know what bridges are. You run up and down them over water and roads.'

'This is the bridge on a ship, dear Simon,' Peggy replies, sounding very posh. 'It's where the Captain sits and some of the others work and make the ship turn. Honest to goodness... '

I feel a bit silly.

'I'm not allowed in there very often,' Peggy continues. 'So I bet you won't be allowed in there either. And just behind the bridge is the cabin where the Captain sleeps. So don't even *think* about going in there.' Captain. Now I've heard of that word.

As she says that, a man comes out and walks towards us. He's dressed in white, holding a drink and has fog coming out of his mouth. Scary! Peggy and I hide behind the turret.

'Quick,' mutters Peggy. 'That's him now. It would be awful if he saw us. Well — you.'

I shiver and make a run for the stairs. I'm pleased to hear Peggy following behind. Hot breath and panting, she eventually catches up with me. I can see her tummy going in and out, in and out.

'My, my, Simon,' she exclaims, her tongue lolling around. 'You're remarkably speedy, aren't you?'

'D'you think he saw us?' I ask, my eyes gleaming and wide with fear.

'I don't think so. He didn't shout after us, did he?' Peggy tries to squeeze into my hiding place, but can't quite manage it. She gets her breath back.

'Oh crikey,' she suddenly gives a little laugh. 'I've just realised what you are.'

I thought she knew what I was? I look at her, confused.

'You're a stowaway.'

'A what-away?'

'Someone who sneaks on board a ship.'

22

Hmm. Not sure I like the sound of that. But I didn't sneak on. I was brought on. By George. I look at the floor. Peggy sees me looking sad.

'Oh, don't worry,' she tries to comfort me. 'It'll be all right. You'll see. Everything's better in the cold light of day.'

We both sit in silence. My nose wrinkles. That pong again.

'Was that you?' I ask.

Peggy looks at the floor.

'It must have been those biscuits I ate before.'

She stands up.

'Come on, let's get you back to George.'

I spring to my feet. Peggy pushes herself up.

'Now, can you remember where it is?'

I find my way back without trouble. Guided by smells. I'm good with smells. Away from one and into another, just as bad.

We stand outside the dark room where the men are sleeping.

'So. Welcome to the HMS Amethyst, little Simon stowaway. D'you like it?'

'It's a bit smelly but, yes, I think I like it. I wonder if I'll be allowed to stay. What d'you think?'

'I've told you, silly Simon, I don't really spend too much time bothering with all of that thinking nonsense. Yesterday is old, tomorrow is brand new and now is all we have. Don't worry.'

And she trots off somewhere, her belly swinging like the beds here in the smelly room. I scamper to where George is sleeping, jump onto a chair and back onto his chest. He doesn't move at all. I close my eyes and hope the only pictures I see are nice ones and not any bad, scary ones.

'Now is all we have, now is all we have.' I feel the comforting rise and fall of George's chest and purr myself to sleep.

7/ Cold and invisible

I open my eyes. I'm not sure where I am, but the smell of humans soon reminds me, followed by the sound of them coughing and spluttering awake. George is still fast asleep, his mouth wide open. As the other men stretch and get out of their swinging beds, some of them spot me and call out.

'Hey, what do we have here?' says one.

'I wonder if Peggy's seen this. I bet she'll eat it for breakfast,' another laughs. I'm glad I met Peggy last night otherwise I'd be really scared now.

Some of the men come over. One of them's long and thin with very red hair. Another has brown hair and the other one has no hair at all. I shrink back. I must have got my claws out too because George wakes up with an 'Oww!' banging his head as he does.

'I see you've got yourself a little mate,' the one with no hair chuckles as he prods George.

'I think I had too much beer last night,' George rubs his head and his eyes. 'I was just coming back here and I heard this little fella.' He tries to sit up, but he swings from side to side and lies back instead.

'Awww. Too much heart. That's you George,' the red hair man laughs.

'Aye. And not enough brains,' says the one with no hair. 'What d'you think Cap'n will say?'

'I don't quite know. I didn't really think.' George's eyebrows move close together.

What did Peggy say about me last night? That I think a lot. Not like her. And here's George saying the same thing. How funny.

'Well, you'd better come up with a plan pretty quick, Georgie boy,' no hair man continues. 'He'll be wanting to speak with us in the mess soon.'

'Move out of the way now fellas,' George replies, finally managing to stand up. 'I need the washroom.'

25

Yes, he *really* does, I think.

As I lift my paw up to give myself a morning wash too some of the men sit there rolling paper and putting it in their mouths. They put some fire up to their mouths — why do they do that? — and blow fog out, just like the Captain last night. As I wash, I watch them and wonder why they'd want to hurt themselves. Some of them are quite noisy and shout to each other, but I don't feel as scared now, so long as they don't try to set fire to *my* face too. As I finish washing, I hear a 'clack, clack, clack', turn around and see Peggy peering at me.

'Good morning.' Peggy's tail's wagging. 'I see you've met some of the sailors. Have they been joking with you?'

'Here, Peggy, Peggy,' no hair man calls her over. He's sitting at a table and looks like he has a biscuit. Peggy trots over, her tail wagging even more. She jumps up and sits next to the man.

'And how about your little friend?' the man says to Peggy, rubbing her head.

Peggy smiles at me. 'This is Gurns,' she woofs. 'He's fun.'

I pad over. He strokes me and I purr. My tail's flicking from side to side a little. The man with dark hair puts something in his mouth.

'Oh, give us a smoke, McCunnell,' Gurns asks.

'I'll think about it, Gurns.' McCunnell lights a paper thing in his mouth and fog comes out from it. He puts his face close to mine and breathes all the fog out right into my face. It makes my eyes sting. I'm not sure I like this McCunnell man very much.

'Get away with ya,' Gurns says and pushes McCunnell's arm away from me. I look over at Peggy, but she's too busy eating to notice.

Gurns reaches across the table and gets a large glass jug of water. The red hair man plops some things into the water. They clink as they fall into the jug and some drops splash onto me. I twitch.

'Oh, get all wet did ya?' McCunnell snorts. 'Can't see you enjoying yourself much on here then. Maybe we should throw you overboard. You'd soon get used to the water.'

Maybe he's right. I don't feel so safe now George isn't here and with Peggy having a new friend in food. What am I doing on here

26

anyway? What did Peggy say I was? A stoneaway? And where am I from? Stonecutters Island? A stoneaway. Away from Stonecutters Island. Maybe I should just jump down off Gurns's knee and run to the stairs and through all the gaps and down the big tongue? But what if the big tongue isn't there? Would I be brave enough to jump over the gunwale and splash into the sea and swim, swim, swim?

Gurns has poured some of the water out from the jug into lots of glasses. The tinkles coming from inside the jug and a flash of light catch my eye. I look at the jug and at the things inside bobbing up and down. I can see right through them. I wonder what they are. I think another man sees me looking because he pushes the jug over to me. Gurns looks down at me and I peer up at him.

'Oh, sorry. I bet you're thirsty aren't you? Fetch a dish, McCunnell.'

'Fetch it yourself,' he answers.

Gurns sighs and stands up. As he does, I spring up from his knee and land on the table.

Oh, how I like the jug of water and the tinkling sound coming from inside! I creep over to it as if I'm about to pounce on JoJo's tail. My back's lowered and my whiskers are twitching. I reach the jug and sniff it. It smells of cold. I lift myself up on my back legs, rest my paws onto the jug and look down into it. I can hear something, but I can't really see anything. Then, oh heavens, what am I doing? I reach down with my paw into the water. It's really cold and it really tickles.

I bat my paw and can feel something. It makes a sound against the side of the jug. I twist my paw around and fish out the cold thing I can feel and hear, but can't really see. It plops from out of my paw and lands onto the table, slithering as it does.

All the men explode with laughter. Apart from McCunnell. He just sits there, but Peggy gives a little bark and smiles at me.

'I think we've got ourselves a fisherman, Ginger,' Gurns says to red hair man, lifting me up and putting me back on his knee.

George comes back in, all dressed and smelling nice.

'Have I missed something?'

'Not half.' Ginger laughs. 'Think we've got ourselves an entertainer. Do it again,' he says to me.

27

So, more for George's benefit than anything, I put my paw back into the water again and scoop out a… whatever it is.

Gurns rubs my head. 'Well done, you,' he smiles, his eyes shining. It really isn't so difficult. I don't understand why they can't do it. Maybe they don't like the things in there, so why do they put them in then? 'What's he called,' Gurns asks.

'Simon,' George tells him. 'His name is Simon.'

I jump down from the table. That's right. My name is Simon.

8/ Time to explore

Peggy comes over to me. 'Don't worry,' she licks my face. 'I would have jumped over to rescue you if mean McCunnell had thrown you overboard. Come on,' she mutters, and clack, clacks out.

We run through the sleeping room and back out to where the stairs are.

'This way,' Peggy half trots, half waddles.

We duck in between the thick, thick chain and another turret until we get right to the back of the boat. We dart — well, I dart, Peggy pushes herself — through many pairs of legs in white flappy trousers all walking quickly and running up stairs, busy, busy.

'This is the stern,' Peggy explains. 'When we're out at sea, sometimes I sit here and watch the white frothy water path we leave behind us. It's awfully good fun. It's also where I do, you know… '

She looks down.

'Where you do what?' I ask her, cocking my head.

'You know, my um… ' Peggy puts her head right up to mine. 'My business,' and she makes a little squatting motion.

'I'll bet back home you just go wherever you like?' she continues.

She's right; I did go wherever I wanted. Even the places I got chased away from.

'Well, on here you need to be much more considerate where you go about doing your, er, business,' she gives a little cough. 'Otherwise you get into the most awful trouble.'

I nod. But I still don't know what she means by considerate business. It sounds very posh. A bit like Peggy.

Peggy shakes herself. 'Anyway, let's continue with the tour.'

We run up some steps leading to the middle of the boat.

'This part is called the quarterdeck,' Peggy tells me. There are lots of sailors all working hard, scrubbing and cleaning. They look very nice in white. The sun's shining down as they work. We scamper down the steps and back to the stern.

'This way. I want to show you one of my favourite places.'

We come to a space full of boxes and lots of other things. It makes me want to explore.

'This is the stowage,' Peggy explains. 'It's where the sailors put everything they need. I curl up and sleep in here sometimes.' She clambers into a battered box. There's a large, chewed stick inside it. 'That's where I was before I smelt you last night.'

We both sniff around before we pad back to the smelly place where the men are.

'Let's run through it quickly,' she suggests.

Some of the men call out after us, 'Here Peggy, hey Simon,' but we don't stop. Instead we get to a place that's very hot indeed.

'This is the engine room. When the boat is out at sea, all these parts move and it gets very smoky and it's frightfully noisy. I don't much like it here. Come on.'

We pass through more doorways until we come to a big room. A room that has lots and lots of tables in it. It smells totally different to anywhere else on the ship. The smells in this room are yummy and make my mouth water.

'This is the mess deck where they eat their food,' Peggy tells me. Some sailors are sitting down as we pass through.

'Oh, I've just realised. I bet you're starving, aren't you?' Peggy asks me. 'Where are my manners? Let me take you to my most favourite place of all. It really is first rate.'

The yummy smell gets stronger as we scamper through what she tells me is a galley. It's only when Peggy nudges me with her nose and yaps at me to keep moving I realise I'm standing still with my nose in the air, imagining the taste of those yummy smells.

'Just a bit further now. This is it.'

I look all around me, but can't see anything.

'Look up.' Peggy points with a paw.

When I do, I see a large friendly face beaming back at us behind an opening.

'Hullo, Peggy,' the face says. 'My, my, what do we have here?'

I look at Peggy. Her tongue's hanging right out. 'This is the stores,' she drools. 'It's like a shop.' And she gives a large bark, her tail wagging.

The friendly face throws Peggy something and she starts to gobble it up. The human taps his hand on the ledge. I suppose it's for me to jump up. I spring up and land on it perfectly.

'Hello, sailor,' the friendly face says. So am I a sailor now too? 'You're awfully pretty aren't you?'

I purr and rub my head against his hand, my tail sticking straight up. I like this man.

'I'm Pauloni. Let's see what we've got for you, shall we?'

He disappears for a second before coming back with a small tin. He opens it and it's full of little fish all packed inside, all stopped.

'Pilchards,' Pauloni says.

He scoops them out onto a plate and I eat them all up, yum, yum, yum. I'm so hungry I've forgotten all about Peggy. I lick my lips and look down at her.

She's looking sad.

'None for me?' she barks.

'Oh, Peggy. Hey girl, good girl.' Pauloni beckons her over. She puts her front paws up to the ledge, licking his hand and wagging her tail as he strokes her, all thoughts of food soon forgotten.

We hear a loud whistle coming from the mess deck. Peggy instantly jumps back down and sets off, her tail still wagging. What else can I do but follow her?

'Bye, sailors,' Pauloni calls after us.

We both run into the mess deck at the same time. There are lots of men sitting there and one man standing up. There's no fog coming from his mouth now, but I recognise him as the Captain. He turns round, sees Peggy and then he sees me.

His face drops.

HMS Amethyst
Photo from the PDSA (People's Dispensary for Sick Animals)

9/ Get a job

I look at the floor. I don't know where to put myself or what to do. Maybe I should run now, although if I splash into the sea Peggy would only come and get me anyway. Peggy! Maybe she can help me. I look at her.

'What shall I do?' I mew as I give myself another clean.

She doesn't have time to answer because the Captain snaps instead, 'Who's responsible for this?' He looks around and all the men go very quiet.

George stands up.

'Me, sir.'

'He was drinking, Captain,' a voice pipes up. It's McCunnell.

'Drinking?' the Captain snaps in a loud, scary voice.

George coughs and looks at the floor. 'I had some leave so I thought— '

'Thought what?' the Captain booms. 'That you would bring an illegal on board? Whatever next! Leave the thinking to me, lad.'

Peggy's tail is right between her legs now. I can smell something I know again.

The Captain's standing very straight. He looks very smart in his white uniform. His buttons are even shinier than the ones I've seen before. He marches over to me and Peggy. I think he's going to pick me up. Instead he bends down in front of Peggy.

'What d'you make of this, Peggy? Friend or foe?'

Peggy licks his hand and wags her tail. She comes over and lies down right next to me. She nuzzles my nose and rests a paw on my back. I let out a purr. The best purr I've *ever* purred. I look up at the Captain. He's looking right back at me and Peggy. I let out another purr. The Captain smiles. I let out one more purr and close my eyes. I can feel my chest pounding, but Peggy's lying right next to me, making me feel all warm.

I half expect to be picked up and thrown — sploosh — right overboard. But nothing happens, so instead I open my eyes again, blinking as I do.

The Captain stands up, looks back at the sailors and points to me and Peggy.

'And there was I thinking cats and dogs were enemies. Perhaps there's a lesson for all of us.'

The Captain turns back to me. I give my best miaow.

'Well, well,' he says. 'It seems like we have another sailor on board,' and all of the men laugh.

'I don't know why *you're* laughing,' the Captain addresses George. 'You're on deck duties for the next thirty days.'

'Aye, aye, sir,' George replies. His smile goes upside down.

I realise my ears are flattened right down, so I spring them up again and walk slowly over to the Captain. He bends down to stroke me.

'You remind me of my Monty back home,' he smiles. 'A most beautiful creature. What's your name?'

'I called him Simon, sir,' George pipes up.

'Ah, Simon. Well, welcome aboard HMS Amethyst. Now, I don't know if you know this, but everyone on board this ship has a job to do. I'm the Captain. And a fine one at that.'

All the men let out another laugh.

'And your friend Peggy there... ' Peggy wags her tail at hearing her name. 'Well, Peggy can smell the enemy coming from one hundred steps.'

And I can smell her coming from two hundred, I think to myself.

'So, if you're going to stay on board the Amethyst, this fine ship, you can jolly well look after her like everyone else. Now, what job shall I give you?'

He thinks for a moment. 'As of today, I order you become our rat catcher, Seacat Simon.'

Seacat Simon. I like the sound of that. And chasing after rats sounds like fun. I wouldn't mind running around this ship and doing that.

'You see, we have a huge rat problem on this ship. They just keep coming and coming. So you… ' he looks right at me now, 'From now on it's *your* job to catch as many of them as you can. And kill them.'

I'm not sure what he means by that, but it sounds less fun than just playing with and chasing them.

'Stop them in their tracks,' the Captain continues. 'And stop them eating all of our supplies.'

Stop them? I think I know what he means now. He means to stop them like Chairman stopped JoJo.

I swallow hard, but a little bit of pilchard comes up. I don't much like the thought of *stopping* anything. Not at all. I don't much like the rats that live back where I'm from, but that doesn't mean that I want to see them *stopped.*

Peggy must notice I've gone from sad to happy to sad again because she comes over. 'Fret not, dear Simon,' she mutters. 'We'll work something out.'

We both lie down as the Captain goes over to join the rest of the men. He starts to speak to them, but I'm not really listening. I'm shaking too much and my fur is quivering all over.

'Permission to speak, sir?' A man who's balancing a line of hair on his lip puts his hand up.

'Yes?' the Captain answers.

'What's our next mission?'

'Tomorrow we head to the Straits, to protect British interests and serve king and country.'

'Aye, sir.' The man who is balancing the hair sits down.

'Back to work,' the Captain commands.

The men all stand at the same time, raise their hands to touch the side of their heads, make a clicking noise with their shoes and file out. I've never seen so many humans doing the same thing at the same time before.

'That includes you two,' the Captain remarks, glancing at me and Peggy.

Peggy sits up and troops out. I follow close behind.

'Well, I don't know about you, but I fear it may be snooze time for Peggy,' she yawns. 'It's all been awfully exciting so far, hasn't it?'

I'm too awake to even think about wanting to close my eyes. Besides, my heart's still pounding about the job the Captain's given to me. We trot through the lower deck and reach the place where Peggy likes to sleep. She settles herself on the floor and rests her head on a paw. I turn round and round, but I don't really want to lie down.

'Stop pacing around,' Peggy snorts. 'What's the matter?'

'I don't think I want to do my job,' I mew sadly.

'None of us *want* to work, Simon,' Peggy replies. 'But it's something we must all do you know. To serve king and country and all that.'

But I don't have a king. I know what they are and what they do and that they live in faraway places, but I know I don't have one. I don't belong to a king. I don't really belong to anyone.

'No,' I whisper. 'I mean I don't want to do that... thing with the rats.'

'Kill them, you mean?' Peggy laughs. 'Oh dear, dear, little Simon. What are you? A mouse? Honest to goodness.'

I know I'm not a mouse. I'm a me! But a me who doesn't want to stop rats.

'D'you like rats, Simon?' Peggy looks at me.

'I don't know. Where I live — where I used to live — I used to see them and they used to see me, but we'd play away from each other.'

'There's good and bad in every one of us Simon... '

I'm not sure there's any bad in me. And definitely not in JoJo. Maybe Chairman has both our bads.

'Good and bad everywhere,' she continues. 'But in rats. Urgh. All they are is bad. They like to eat everything.'

'Well, what's so bad about that? I like to eat everything.' Almost. I look at Peggy's belly sticking out from underneath her and am going to say she likes to eat everything too, but I don't.

'Yes,' Peggy lifts her head up. 'But rats run over all the pots and sacks and any food in the galley and make everyone poorly. They enjoy it as well.'

'Why?'

'I don't know. But they like it.'

'So you really think I should stop rats?' I ask Peggy.

'Not stop them, Simon. Kill them. Make them die.'

I shudder again.

'I don't know if I can.' My whiskers droop down and I look at the floor.

'Fear not, my little friend. For I have a plan.'

My eyes brighten up at the sound of that one.

'Do you? Do you really?' I look at her.

Peggy gives a little cough and shuffles around again. 'Well, I haven't quite worked it out yet. As I've said, I'm a doer and you're a thinker. But I'm quite sure that, with a bit of thinking and a lot of doing, we'll fight those evil rats and we shall win.'

And with that, Peggy closes her eyes and goes straight to sleep.

I lift my leg up and give myself a lick. It helps me to think sometimes when I do that. I think perhaps I have a *lot* of licking ahead of me.

Simon on board HMS Amethyst
Photo from the PDSA

10/ Soapy fun

Peggy's snoring in her box so I creep out. After I've been on the stern to do my business — I know what Peggy means now, I've watched her and smelt it — I run under the huge chain and scamper up the stairs onto the quarterdeck.

There are lots of men up here. Some of them are whistling, some of them are rubbing the boat making it all clean and some of them are using brooms like the one the woman in the alley chased me and Uboat away with. There are soap suds everywhere with lots of different coloured lights wiggling in them. The soap suds go 'pop' when I bat them with my paw. I spy George and run over to him, my feet slipping out from under me as I run through the soapy suds.

He wipes his brow as I reach him, bends down and gives me a stroke. I rub against him. I want him to know I like him, but also that I like being in this place as well. On this ship. The Amethyst. What a funny name.

'My, my Simon, that was close, eh? Maybe I shouldn't drink all that beer in future. It doesn't half get me into a lot of trouble.'

I walk in between his legs and purr, happy that he seems happy.

'Good job Lieutenant Griffiths liked you. Now, if you can just start killing those darned rats we'll all be happy.'

'Hey, George,' a sailor calls over. 'How about we stick your little friend on the other end of one of these,' and he holds up one of the brooms. 'We'd get this deck clean in no time.'

My ears go right back.

'Ah, put a sock in it, Conway,' George shouts over to him.

'I'll sock you in half a jiffy,' Conway calls back.

Why are they talking about socks? George must notice my ears as he says, 'Ah, don't worry about him. They don't mean what they say,' and he strokes my back again.

I lick my paw and give myself a wash as I sit and carry on watching George and the other sailors for a while. I don't see Ginger or Gurns or McCunnell. Not that I want to see McCunnell, thank you very much. There's something about him I don't like.

I hear an angry shout, and see McCunnell rushing towards me with a broom. I feel all my fur stick up as I spring to my feet and dash off. I scamper down the stairs and hear a yell behind me. As I turn round, I see McCunnell slip right over and fall on his bottom. I hear howls of laughter from the men cleaning the deck as I reach the bottom of the stairs and turn to run up the — starboard — side. Yes, I'm getting better at these names now.

Under a rope, in between here, over a… thing… and now I'm at the front — the bow. There are some sailors up here too. One of them's looking at a huge bit of paper with all sorts of squiggly lines on it and another is scratching his head.

I don't quite know what to do next, so I just stand there and stare for a while then decide to explore the bridge, even though Peggy said I shouldn't. I trot through a doorway and take a look around. There's lots of paper, paper everywhere. Oh, I want to jump on it all. I really, really want to lie on it, it looks so… mmm. I'm just about to jump on some of the paper when the door opens. It's the Captain. Oh dear!

11/ Playtime

The Captain doesn't notice me at first. Instead he sits down and looks at all the paper. He's holding something in his hand and moving it around. Lots of marks appear on the paper as he moves his hand.

I give a little mew and he looks up.

'Ah, Seacat Simon. Managed to catch any of those pesky rats yet? Good. Good.'

I pad over to him.

'Just making some plans for when we finally make a move tomorrow. Oh gosh, I've just thought of something. You're not a spy are you? Sent by the enemy?'

What on *earth* is he talking about?

'I expect you want a drink?'

The Captain gets up and goes through the door. I follow him and we step into a large room. It's very warm and nice in here, like a big hiding place. I can see a table and lots of things on shelves and comfy things for me to curl up on.

'Make yourself at home,' the Captain says and turns around as I jump onto his bed. 'Ah, I see you already have. Jolly good.'

There's a white and gold hat upside down on his bed so I get into it. He fetches a glass and a jug like the one before with the water in, only this one contains something dark. He looks over to me.

'Whiskey? No, of course not.'

He fetches me some water and pours it into a cup before pouring some of the dark water into a glass. He puts them both onto a table next to the bed. I notice there are some things in like the ones I fished out earlier. I can see them better now. Maybe I should put my paw in?

The Captain sits next to me, reaches for his drink and knocks it back. I get up out of his hat, pad over to the table, put my nose into the cup and lap up the water.

'I say, have you ever seen these?' and he pulls something out of his starboard pocket. They're like very smooth painted red rocks, with dots on every side. I get back into his hat next to him on the bed.

'These are called dice,' he says, 'And just one is called a die,' he adds, polishing only one on his jacket.

I swallow. I don't like the sound of this.

'I use it sometimes when I'm caught between the devil and the deep blue sea.'

Hmmm. I know where the deep blue sea is, but where's the devil?

'Darned useful for making decisions sometimes, this is,' he continues. 'Sunk more than one U-boat with this, I have.'

Oh dear. This is getting worse.

The Captain throws the hard thing across the room. It rolls and rolls before coming to a stop. Not a stop. It just doesn't roll anymore.

What does he want me to do now? Find my friend Uboat, sink him and then die?

I look at him. He looks back at me. He stands up and pours himself another drink of dark water.

'Ah, that's a shame. My Monty used to run after a die all the time.'

I've heard that some me's do that. But that isn't really, um, me.

The Captain's muttering. 'Used to pretend I was playing poker dice with him.'

What is this? Some kind of game?

I decide if he throws it again I'll jump down after it. I know if I was a dog I'd probably just run over, pick it up and drop it at his feet without thinking. I've seen them do that before. But I'm not a dog! I'm sure that's what Peggy would do if she was here. Actually, I bet she would just eat it. I think of JoJo and how he used to love running around after a ball. He would have done it.

The Captain picks up the thing again, sits back down on the bed and rolls it between his fingers. I can smell his breath and I notice his eyes are quite red.

'One for sorrow. Two for joy. Three for a girl, four for a boy...
I hope you're a boy, Simon,' he chuckles. 'Did George check for that?
I knew you were as soon as I saw you, but George, bet it didn't even
cross his mind. Now, where were we? Ah yes. Five for a wish. I wish.
I wish I was back home in England, that's what I wish. Six for a... I
can't remember what six is for.'

It drops out of his fingers and, as it does so, I knock it with my
paw onto the floor. The Captain looks down.

'Six!' He exclaims. 'Goodness. I'll make a player out of you yet. And with a pokerface like that I'm sure we'll make an absolute killing.'

Gulp. That word again.

'Here, let's try it again.'

He gives the die back to me and once again I knock it onto the floor with a paw.

'Oh, my goodness. I don't believe it. A six again. Talk about luck.'

I look at the dots on the die and back at the Captain. Now, I'm not really very good with numbers, but I'm sure something has just happened. I'm not sure what.

The Captain is sitting on his bed pouring himself another drink.

'This is incredible. I'll just… ' He knocks the dark drink back. 'I'll just… ' He falls backwards onto his bed. His eyes close. That snoring noise.

I look around. I quite like it in here. In fact, I like it in here a lot. There's no smell like in the lower deck. Well, there is. A different smell. The smell of the Captain's breath is in the room, but it makes me feel quite sleepy. Maybe that's why he… yes, it makes me feel very sleepy indeed. I think I'll, I'll get back into his hat and… that's it, round and round and down and… aah...

****

I open my eyes with a jolt. Oops, I've been asleep. It's quite dark in here, but it just means I can see that the Captain has gone. He won't be wearing his hat though because I'm still in it. I wonder where he's gone. I wonder what Captains even *do* apart from walk around and tell people what to do and make fog and drink dark water and roll a die.

I get up, stretch and jump off the bed. I think I'll go down to the shop and see if I can get any food. I go over to the door, but it's closed. I sit back down. At least the floor is nice and warm.

Soon I hear footsteps outside so I cry out. Sometimes humans tell me to shut up when I make a noise so maybe they will now, and when they come in I can escape! I make a noise again. The footsteps stop and the door opens. It's a man I don't recognise.

'Evening, Simon,' the man says. 'The Captain said you would be in here. He told me to bring you this,' and he puts down a plate with some lovely food on. Then he puts his hand out to me. 'I'm Weston. First Lieutenant. Pleased to meet you.' What does he want me to do with his hand?

I stare at him until he walks out before I turn to the plate. I sniff it and then have a little nibble. Yum. I eat some and then leave some. I often do that, even when it tastes very nice. Like now.

Weston has left the door open, so I skip out and run back, back, down the stairs, along the ship and get to the stern. The stars are twinkling above my head. I run into the lower deck, wrinkle my nose and find George on his swinging bed. He's sitting up as best as he can in the little hiding place. Just like the Captain, he's holding something in his hand and making marks on paper.

'Where've you been, Simon?' he asks, rubbing my head. 'I heard you got into a spot of bother with old McCunnell today? He's a bit slippery that one,' and George laughs to himself. I jump up on his knee. 'Ah, careful,' he says. 'I'm just writing a letter back home. I miss home.' He points to a picture of some humans. I look back at him and his eyes are all wet.

12/ Off to sea

Peggy and I have just been to see Pauloni. He gave us some nice titbits. Then he shooed us away because he said he had lots to do as today is a big, big day. I know what 'day' is, it means when it's not dark time, but I'm not sure how one day can be bigger than another.

The sailors are running around all over the place, busy, busy. I notice George's eyes aren't wet anymore. Maybe if he makes the deck all soapy and clean and then rubs his head it stops them from getting wet? Maybe it's just when he makes wiggly lines on paper that that happens, so perhaps he just shouldn't put wiggly lines on paper?

Peggy says it's because we're going to sea soon and that's why everyone's busy, so it's best if we just hide. She said I'll like it when the ship sets sail. I've seen ships and boats come in and out of the harbour, so I know what it's like to watch a ship when I'm on the dock, but not what it's like when I'm on a ship and not on the dock.

I'm going to go from where I'm from to where I'm not from, I suppose. I wonder if I'll see green birds like Uboat told me about. I can feel a flutter in my belly, but I don't really know what it is because I'm not hungry. Not after having a yummy titbit anyway.

I tell Peggy.

'Maybe you have butterflies in your stomach?' she laughs as she clambers out of her box in the stowage.

I don't, I really don't. The last time I ate one of those, it really tickled and I could barely breathe. It was almost as bad as when I sometimes sicky up a ball of my own black fur.

'Or maybe it's the rats,' Peggy continues. 'I've seen them again, running around all over the food in the kitchen. All over the rice and where they make the bread. So have you come up with a plan as to how to put a stop to all their beastly activity?'

'Well… ' I've been trying my best not to think about it. I was hoping a picture might come into my head when I closed my eyes as

I went to sleep on George last night. 'We could always maybe try… talking to them and ask them to stop?'

Peggy throws her head back and wuffs. 'Ha, ha, woof, ha, Simon. That really is the most awfully mad idea I've heard for a long, long time.' She laughs and wuffs some more. 'Have you ever tried to reason with a rat?'

No, I haven't. Back where I'm from they used to leave me alone and I used to leave them alone.

'No,' I tell Peggy. 'Me and JoJo… we just used to play away from them.'

'Well, let me tell you, they really are the most horrid, sneaky creatures. The Captain said we must kill them and that is what we shall do.'

I look at the floor and feel a flutter in my stomach. A slightly different one this time.

'Oh.'

'No 'oh-ing' about it. Dear, oh dear,' and she shakes her head a little. Some spit flies from her mouth onto my head so I have to lick and clean myself straight away. I think it's worse than when she parps at me!

A huge noise makes us both jump. It's as if all the men in the world have shouted at us at once. The room starts to shake too.

'That's the engine!' exclaims Peggy, wagging her tail. 'We must be setting off. Wuff, wuff, what fun!'

I run outside with Peggy following not so close behind. Both of us have to squeeze past the huge, huge chain because it's moving and rattling. It looks like a big, big snake and the sound of it hurts my ears. Now the whole ship seems to be shaking. It's very noisy indeed. Rattle, rattle, shake, shake.

'Quick, let's run up to the bow,' barks Peggy. Up we scamper, right onto the bow. I look down and see the big tongue has gone. There's nothing now between the ship and the port, my home. This is it. My heart jumps and thumps. I couldn't go home now even if I wanted to. Could I jump into the sea and swim back?

No. As I think, I realise I don't even want to. This is the start of my new adventure. The start of me being brave.

13/ Best laid plans

I feel the whole ship start to move, except it feels as if someone or something is pulling me by my bottom. We're moving, but it feels as if we're moving bottomwards instead of forwards. How funny.

As we start to move, I look down onto the dock and can see a group of humans waving at us. There are some children playing too. They're playing with a ball and they're throwing it and trying to get it into a box. I see a picture of me and JoJo and of how we used to play that game as well. The picture changes from a game into a plan and I feel a sudden burst of happy inside me.

I look up and see some birds following the back of the boat. They're all tweeting, but I can't tell what they're saying. I'm flying away from where I'm from even faster than they are.

'Bye bye, where I'm from. Bye bye, horrible Chairman. Bye bye, JoJo,' I mew quietly. I stare straight ahead and try to blink the water out of my eyes. It's just splashes from the sea. We're moving up and down too. It's as if the whole ship has turned into a big swinging bed. I'm moving from side to side, up and down. It feels very odd.

I can feel the breeze and I listen to the ship hum and rattle. It smells all fresh. I'm going somewhere new, but I don't know where. It's more exciting than scary. I only wish JoJo was here too. We could be having a new adventure together. This new adventure. This new life.

Spray splashes in my eyes and a little on my nose. I lick it. It tastes a little bit like the stopped fish. I wouldn't want to drink much of it. It's a bit windy and I shiver, from the breeze or from being excited, I don't know. Now we're sailing right in between the walls on either side of the harbour. Right through them until we reach the big, big sea. The clear blue water ahead, the bright blue sky above.

I don't think I've ever moved this fast before, not even when I've had to run away from scary things. My ears are right back, but that's because of the wind. This is fun, fun, fun! Peggy smiles at me.

'Are you enjoying yourself?' she asks.

'Oh, yes,' I reply. 'I could stand here for all of this big day.'

'So could I. But I'm afraid we both have some work to do. All play and no work means... well, I don't really know what it means, but come on.'

We run back to the stern, but it's still very noisy and now it's quite smelly too so we run up to the quarterdeck and hide.

'I think I've had a picture,' I say to Peggy.

She looks at me slightly puzzled. 'You mean you've been thinking? So have I. I've been thinking about food.'

'No. A plan.'

'Jolly good. What is it, dear Simon? Do tell... '

So, over the noise of the engine and under the bright sky, I tell her.

'By Jove, I think you've got it!' she exclaims. 'I knew if we put our heads together we could come up with something.'

Now it's my turn to look puzzled. I don't remember putting my head next to hers when I came up with my plan.

We head back to the stores again. I'm on the counter, walking up and down and turning around as Pauloni strokes me. Peggy jumps up and puts her paws on the counter. Pauloni keeps giving us lots of titbits, but we're not eating them. Every time he turns around to fetch us some more, we drop them onto the floor. He's talking to us both.

'Aren't you both lovely? Yes you are! You with your licky tongue and you with your gorgeous fur. It would make someone a most fabulous coat,' he laughs and gives me another stroke. 'Just teasing! I don't know what I'd do on here without such good friends to keep me company.'

I purr as Pauloni carries on talking to me and Peggy.

'And I can tell you like being on here,' he says to me. 'Yes, you do.'

Peggy gives me a look and gets down from the counter. I notice she gathers up some biscuits and other treats in her mouth.

'Try not to eat any,' I whisper to her.

'I'll try,' she mumbles, her mouth full, and she trots off, but I can tell she's looking a little sad. Shortly afterwards, she comes back. When she does, I jump down from the counter too. Between us we both carry all the yummy bits of food away. It takes a long time.

'Well done,' I smile at Peggy.

'Yes,' she answers. 'And I didn't even eat any either. Well, perhaps just a nibble… '

After Peggy and I have had a snooze, we meet again in the stowage. It's nice and warm in here now. She clambers out of her box and looks at it. 'I hope this works,' she remarks.

We break up the biscuits into small pieces with our paws. Then, making sure all the men are snoring, we trot through the lower deck and through to the galley, carrying the small pieces in our mouths. We drop some of the broken bits onto the floor, run back and fetch some more. We drop bits of food all the way, right through the lower deck and along to the stowage.

'Like Hansel and Gretel,' Peggy mutters.

'What's that?' I ask her.

'A fairy story I heard someone tell some children once,' she answers. 'Or maybe I saw it.'

I don't really know what she means. Never mind. In the stowage, Peggy drags her sleeping box over near the door. Between us, we tip the box over so we can get in it from the side instead of having to climb into it. We drop more bits of food from the doorway all the way to the box. Peggy hides behind it while I hide near the doorway. It's like we're playing a game. Only a game where we have to wait for a long time.

It makes me want to sleep. I look over to see where Peggy's hiding. I can hear her snoring.

'Peggy, wake up,' I miaow loudly.

'Sorry,' she mumbles. 'I was miles away.'

No she wasn't! She's right here with me. Dogs are very odd.

We wait and we wait. I tell Peggy to make a noise every so often so I know she hasn't gone to sleep again. After my eyes have closed and opened, closed and opened, I hear a sound. Quiet at first before getting louder, a snuffling and a squeaking and then a scrabbling of feet. I shrink back and try to hide some more.

Suddenly, I see not one, but two rats. Pink noses, like mine; pink feet, not like mine; and long thin tails, not like mine. They smell of not very niceness too. The first rat is very big. Very big indeed. His eyes are very small though. The rat behind him is smaller. They both come in closer, nibbling at the broken biscuits, moving forwards, forwards until they're right next to the box.

Blam! I spring forwards and jump in front of the doorway, blocking their way. At the same time, Peggy stands up and knocks the box over. It falls forwards and traps both rats inside.

We've done it!

Peggy and the crew
Photo from Lieutenant Commander Stewart Hett

Peggy and the crew
Photo from Lieutenant Commander Stewart Hett

14/ Caught

I can hear the two rats running round and round inside the box.

'What do we do now?' I whisper to Peggy.

'Why, we wait of course,' she answers.

'What? For them to… *stop? Really* stop?' I look at her.

'Yes,' she replies.

Gulp.

'And then we do it again and catch some more,' Peggy continues.

I can't help but feel a little bit sorry for them.

'Maybe we could just talk to them?' I suggest.

Peggy shakes her head. 'Tsk. Oh dear, oh dear.'

'How long will it take for them to stop moving?' I ask Peggy.

'I have absolutely no idea,' she answers. 'A few days, I suppose.'

I try and think how long that might be. It sounds like it could be for a long time. 'And d'you really want to sleep in here when they are… doing that in the box?' I don't think I would like to do that. Not at all.

'Hmm. Mmm,' she answers. 'I think I'd rather have my box back.'

I give a little tap on the box. The rats stop shuffling around.

I put on my best, scary voice. 'Hello, rats.'

Peggy looks at me. After a pause one of the rats replies in a thin, squeaky voice.

'Yeess…?'

'What would you like to do? Would you like to stay in the box until bad things happen to you, or d'you want to talk to us?'

The rats shuffle and mutter.

'We will talk to you. Yeesss,' the same rat squeals.

I wave to Peggy and she bites at a corner of the box and lifts it up a little. As the two rats crawl out from under it, she stands in front of the doorway so they can't escape.

'Who are you? Sss,' the big rat looks at me, its black eyes squinting.

'I am the king of all the rat catchers,' I reply. 'Who are you?'

'I am Mao Tse Tung, leader of the Rats Army,' the big rat answers.

'We could have left you in there, you know,' I say. 'I could catch all of you rats, if I wanted to.' I puff out my little chest to make myself bigger.

'Just try it,' the other rat sneers, but Mao Tse Tung flicks him with his tail.

'Would you like me to catch all of you?' I continue. 'I'm very good.'

Mao Tse Tung shakes his head.

'I have a plan. If we promise to give you some food, d'you promise to stop running around all over our ship?'

'And why would we do that? Ssss.' Mao Tse Tung hisses again.

'Because we let you go instead of leaving you trapped. And because if you make all the men ill then there won't be any more food. And if there isn't any food there won't be any of *you*.' I'm quite enjoying all this pretending.

Mao Tse Tung lifts his head in the air and gives a little sniff. 'OK,' he answers. 'Rat's promise. Ssss.'

'Is that a deal?' Peggy asks him.

Mao Tse Tung looks at the floor. 'Deal,' he replies finally.

I hear Peggy give a little sigh. But I don't want them to stop. I want to let them go. Chairman could have let JoJo go. But he didn't. I don't want to be like Chairman.

Peggy shuffles to one side and the rats scamper off, their tails between their eight little legs.

'You sounded awfully funny,' Peggy says, licking my nose.

58

'Funny or scary? I wanted to sound like a king.' I give myself a little scratch.

'I'm not sure. I don't know what a king sounds like.' Peggy lies down. 'D'you think that will stop the rats from running all over the food and making the men ill?'

'I don't know,' I answer. 'Do you?'

'I've said it before and I'll say it again. You can't reason with a rat,' Peggy mutters.

'Maybe you can if you're king of the rat catchers,' I purr. 'We'll just have to see. But it means we'll have to do a lot of running around and getting bits of food. No more eating everything.'

'I suppose so,' she replies sadly.

'And at least you've got your box back,' I smile.

She puts her head inside. 'Although it's most awfully smelly.'

She parps so much, it's always smelly. Maybe she can't smell her own parps!

We lie on the stern and look out. The ship's going up and down, but I like the way it makes me feel. The sky and the sea are all I see. I don't know if big-small is a word but that's how I feel. Peggy wuffs at me to show me the white waves coming out from behind the ship as it cuts through the water. It looks like a long white tail.

'Would you still jump in after me if I fell in?' I ask Peggy.

'Oh, yes,' she replies.

'Even though the ship would be moving quickly away from us?'

'Um. I hadn't really thought about that. Maybe if I barked very hard they would hear us and come back.'

Hmmm. I'm not so sure. It's still quite noisy. So noisy that I don't even hear the footsteps of McCunnell and another sailor creeping towards us.

'Thought you were supposed to be catching rats,' McCunnell snarls.

Suddenly, before I even have a chance to spring away, he leaps forwards and grabs me. My little legs dangle down between his arms and he's holding me tight, tight. Then he dangles me right over the side of the ship.

Peggy barks and barks, but he doesn't seem to notice. I can see the water just below me and feel the wind as the ship races through the water.

'D'you fancy a swim?' he laughs. 'I could throw you right overboard and nobody would ever know… '

I don't like this. Not at all. My heart's beating fast, fast. It's dark as I close my eyes and then bright as I open them again, staring as the sea rushes past me below my paws. Peggy runs over, growling, and I hear her bite into McCunnell's leg. He goes to kick her away, but she keeps hold with her teeth.

The other man just stands there. 'Eh,' he says eventually. 'Leave them be.'

McCunnell steps back and drops me onto the deck. Peggy lets go of his leg. 'Grrr,' he says at us and we both shoot off under the stairs, run round the place of the huge chain and to the other side of the ship. We're both panting and my eyes are full of water.

'My goodness, are you all right?' Peggy asks me. 'I really tried to bite as hard as I could, you know. He didn't even taste very nice either.'

'Thank you, Peggy. That wasn't very nice at all. I really thought he was going to throw me over.'

'Maybe we should go back to Mao Tse Tung and tell him to attack McCunnell in his sleep,' Peggy pants.

I wonder if having a picture of a bad thing happening to someone bad is good or not? And didn't Peggy say there was good and bad everywhere and in all of us? So there must be some good in McCunnell somewhere. But there was none in Chairman.

My pictures are stuck between good and bad and the open sea. I blink, twitch my nose and decide to go to the bow. And also to keep away from McCunnell as much as possible from now on. As I stand there, with the wind whistling through my ears, the Captain appears.

'Ah, the open sea,' he says to me and gives me a little stroke. 'I only wish my dear Monty could have joined me out here. You've already seen more things than he ever has.' We stand on the bow for a long time. Sometimes he puts things into his mouth and fog comes out, but I'm not scared by it anymore. He also has a very big pair of long, round things that he puts up to his face and then looks around. After a while, he turns and goes back onto the bridge, so I follow him. As I get to the doorway I stop.

'Oh, do come in,' he says. 'You *are* allowed. Captain's orders.'

I trot through the bridge. There are some men in there. One of them is standing beside all the papers. It's the same man who gave me some food and let me go when I was trapped in the Captain's cabin. He did that to me and I did that to the rats. How funny.

'Making good progress are we, Weston?' the Captain asks.

'Aye, sir. We'll be reaching the Malaya Straits right on time.'

'Good. Good. Any reports of any activity?'

'Three ships sighted, sir, but they're not a problem,' another man replies.

'Well, I'll send a message out to them to offer our assistance if needed,' the Captain continues. 'Meanwhile, if anyone needs me, I'll be in my cabin.'

'Very good, sir.'

The Captain enters his cabin, removes his cap and puts it on the end of his bed. I jump up onto it as he pours himself a drink of the dark water. I listen for the clink, but I don't hear anything. Then he lies on the bed next to me. It's very comfy on here and in this cabin. Much more so than in the lower deck with all the other smelly men. And where not very nice McCunnell is of course.

I think I may just stay here for the rest of this big day. And it *has* been a big day too.

15/ Pops with stars

I'm lying under a table in the mess deck with Peggy. George is sitting at the table with Ginger.

'Haven't seen King Rat in the galley for a while,' Ginger says to George. 'Your Simon must have polished him off.'

I don't know about polished. But every night time — I know now it's called that when it isn't day — me and Peggy leave some food that's yummy and food that's not so yummy out near the stern. And when it gets light and the men are all out of their swinging beds and working, the food has all gone. We can smell that Mao Tse Tung has been. Peggy says he is our enemy, but I just think he isn't a friend. Friends and not friends. From and not from. Peggy and George — friends. McCunnell — not friend.

Not that I spend much time on the stern. Peggy likes to watch the white tails, coming out bottomwards, I suppose. I like to be right on the bow, looking out. Can it really be all big, big sea everywhere, all the time?

I even like the noise the ship makes. Sometimes I picture lots and lots of me's, as many as I can, all purring at the same time, but I'm still not very good with numbers, so I end up picturing one big me instead.

My fur's stiff and sticky all of the time too, no matter how often I lick my paw and try to clean myself. Sometimes, when George is having a wash, I sit there and watch as he gets all wet. I like it more now when the splashes land on me.

I'm getting better at fishing the things I can't see out of a jug of water. I do it whenever some of the men like Ginger and Gurns don't look happy. It makes them laugh. It still makes my paws cold though.

As I lie under the table near George's feet — they're not so smelly when he has his big black boots on — Weston comes in. He's often on the bridge helping the Captain and they talk together a lot.

'Simon,' he looks at me and smiles. 'The Captain wants to see you.'

I run alongside him until we get to the bridge. He bends down and rubs my head before I pad into the Captain's cabin. He's sitting in a chair, rolling the die between his fingers, a drink in his other hand.

'Ah, my good cat. Do come in. Everyone treating you well I hope? Good.'

How I wish I could tell him about McCunnell.

'Thought you might want to play a little game,' the Captain says cheerfully.

I jump up onto his knee, almost spilling his drink. Of course I'd like to play a game. I always do. I can't imagine a time when I wouldn't want to run around and play.

'I'm going to throw this again,' he waves the die in front of my face. 'I'm going to roll it three times and if we get a six you can have a lovely treat.'

Oh good. I know what treats are!

'D'you think I can do it?' The Captain laughs. 'Of course I can.'

He leans forwards a little and throws the die onto the floor. It rolls and comes to a stop.

'Oh, darn!' He sits back and slams his knee with his hand. I shuffle further up then, as he stands to collect the die, I drop down to the floor and run over to it. I give it a little sniff and a knock with my paw. As I do so, it rolls to one side.

'I don't believe it!' he exclaims. 'You've done it again. No need to roll it again now. Just wait there a moment,' and he walks quickly out of his cabin.

I sit there, not quite sure what to do. I hope I'm not in trouble. I lick my paw and wash my face as I wait.

The Captain enters again with a big smile, a tin can and a bowl. 'You'll like this,' he beams. 'I got one of the men to get some for you just before we set sail. Have you heard of Lane Crawford?'

I stare at him. What *is* he on about?

'A lovely shop it is. They have goodies from all over the world. English tea, chocolate biscuits.'

He puts the bowl on the floor next to me, sits down and takes something from his pocket. He uses whatever it is to dig into the top of the can. He moves the can round slowly in his hand as he does. He even makes a little squealing noise and puts his hand in his mouth to lick away some of the red that's appeared. But, as he takes the top off the tin, there's a most yummy smell.

'Here,' he says, scooping out some of the contents from the tin into the bowl next to me. 'I'm sure you're going to love this. Whiskas,' he says.

I'm not sure why he says that. I already *have* whiskers and I know they're not brown and they don't smell like this. I stand up and stare at the bowl with the brown food in it. I circle around it slowly, sniffing and letting the smell go up my nose and swim around my head. It smells so yummy it almost makes me feel dizzy. I don't know what it is. What could it be?

Whatever it is, it's most definitely good and not bad. If it was bad then I would just wrinkle my nose and walk away of course. But oh no, it isn't that, it isn't that at all. It's good, good, good! A part of me wants to just put my head right in and eat it all up, but another part of me wants to just sniff and wait and, mmm, sniifff...

Maybe when I put my head in and try it, it won't taste as good as it smells, so then I'll just feel sad. But maybe I could put my head in and take a little nibble and it'd taste even better than the promise of it as it tickles my nose? This most lovely smell coming from the brown food in the bowl in front of me is making my head spin now. One more slow dance around the bowl, a little dip of my head and... Shall I? Shall I do it now?

I put my head right into the bowl, do a big breathe in, feel my tummy go big, stick my tongue out, take a little lick and... Ooh that's the best thing I've ever tasted in my life, much better than the stopped fish back home. My head pops with stars like in the sky at night time and my tongue seems to melt and disappear. I take a mouthful, swallow and feel the best food in the world slip down my throat, into my belly and send a shiver all the way right down to the end of my tail. Another little bite and — oh yes — I feel it right down to the end of each of my paws.

I want to run round and round in circles, jump high, high into the air, get right into the bowl and cover myself with this lovely, yummy brown food. I take another sniff before I have some more. Mmm, just as good. I could eat and eat this until I get as big as Peggy. Bigger. I wonder if she's ever tried this. Or even knows what it is. Maybe I'll tell her. Maybe I won't and just keep it all to myself! And one thing's for sure, Mao Tse Tung is definitely not going to have any.

I look up at the Captain and he is smiling, smiling. Why isn't he eating any of this? I'm sure this brown food is nicer than the brown drink he likes. Another taste and chew and swallow. And another. Shall I eat it all up quickly? I don't know. All I know is this is where I want to be right now, more than anything else. On this ship. With George and with Peggy and the Captain. And this lovely, lovely, yummy brown food in the bowl.

'See,' the Captain says. 'I knew you'd enjoy it.'

16/ Previous life

Peggy and I are playing, even as it gets hotter. We run round and round the ship. I want to chase her, but it's easy to catch up with her, so I get her to chase me instead. She can never catch me though, so sometimes I run slower just so she can. Her tongue's always hanging out as she pants and pants and her tail's wagging, so I know she's happy. My tail doesn't wag when I'm happy. I wonder why hers does and mine doesn't.

As we run and play, I look out across the sea. Far, far away, just where it ends, I can see a dark shape. It looks like a small black cloud has come to sit right on top of the sea.

'Look,' I call out to Peggy. 'I can see something.'

She comes running up to me. 'So can I. I can see the sea.' She snorts.

'No, no. Over there. Look.' I try to get Peggy to see where I'm staring.

She looks and sniffs and looks. Then she shakes her head. 'I think you must be wrong, dear Simon. There really is nothing out there.'

As she says that, Ginger and Gurns appear. Gurns puts his hand above his eyes and squints.

'Malaya,' Ginger cries.

So that's it. It's a place I can see. Land. Called Malaya. I wonder what it's like!

'Are we going to go there?' I ask Peggy.

'I shouldn't think so,' she replies.

That's a shame. It might be fun to see another place. A place where I'm not from. I wonder what the humans would be like in that place. And the birds. And the food too! I stand there and look out at the dark shape. At Malaya. What happens there? Is it more good than bad?

'How d'you know so much, Peggy?' I ask her.

'Because my master told me,' she answers, yawning.

'Lieutenant Griffiths?'

'Heavens, no. I didn't always live on this ship, don't you know.'

'So where *did* you live?' I ask, my ears flicking forward.

'I used to live in a most wonderful big house. There were lots of rooms and comfy beds. And I had lots of toys. My favourite was a blue sock monkey.'

Ah. Monkeys. Uboat said he'd seen them. 'What's a monkey?' I ask.

'They're very soft and cuddly creatures,' Peggy replies. 'My toy monkey was, anyway, so I suppose they are in real life as well. I don't know. I'd love to meet one though. I used to chew and chew my monkey until he only had one ear left. We had a most pretty garden too.'

I look at her. 'And was it just you and your master who lived in the big house?'

'Oh, no. He had a wife and children, and we also had a lovely maid who used to do everything. She would wash and cook and clean. She used to give me lots of nice food all of the time. I'd go for long, long walks with my master. He used to throw me sticks and I'd chase after them, bring them back to him and he'd throw them again.' Peggy's back legs twitch as she tells me this.

'Throw. Run. Catch. Run back. Throw, run, catch, run back…,' she continues.

I close my eyes and I get the picture, I really do. I've seen dogs do that before. I always wonder why they do that when *I* don't want to. It seems a bit silly to me. I know I might do it for the Captain sometimes, but that's just because he seems to like it. Maybe that's why dogs always do it with their masters, to make them happy?

Peggy shakes her head, as if trying to stop herself from falling asleep.

'Anyway,' she continues. 'Something happened to my master and we stopped going out for long walks. The maid still used to feed me but, instead of going out, I just used to run around in the garden.'

'Then what happened?'

'I woke up one day and they weren't there anymore.' Now she looks sad. 'People came and chased me, so I had to run away. Well, not run. Move quite fast. All I had was my monkey.'

I don't really like this story now. It's making me feel sad too.

'And then what?'

'Well, I don't really know. Somebody found me and gave me to the Captain. He brought me and my monkey on board this ship and I've been on here ever since.'

Is that what humans do, I wonder. Do they find us and look after us? Well, that must mean they're good. Mostly good. I think of McCunnell.

'Where's your monkey now?'

'I don't know.' She looks sad again. 'I think the Captain might have lost it or it might have fallen overboard or something.' She stops herself from looking sad and tries to jump on me, but I spring out of her way. I playfully chase her back to her box until she smiles, rolls over, gives a little parp and falls asleep.

I get up and run into the lower deck. I know the sailors are on deck so they won't be asleep, so I give a little jump when I hear, 'Hey, Simon.'

It's Gurns, lying on his swinging bed. He tells me he dreams of his sweetheart back home. I purr as I listen to him. A sweetheart is someone who you like the best. He says he loves her and wants to be with her forever. Love. I wonder what that is. But if it's to do with somebody that you want to be with all the time then it must mean it's a good thing. Love must mean that humans see pictures like me, like when I see JoJo. And love must be something you want to be in forever. So it's nice to be able to close your eyes and be with who you love.

As Gurns tells me about his sweetheart and love and I start to see pictures, I can feel my whiskers droop and my eyes start to close. I don't mean to, I didn't think I wanted to, but it's so hot and I've been so busy today, running and playing and purring. I stretch and yawn and… ahhh…

Purrrrr...

17/ Singapore scare

Behind is the big blue sea, stretching out maybe forever. Above there are some birds that have joined us, flying and tweeting above the ship, as if they're saying hello. Ahead I can see land and buildings getting closer.

We're going to Singapore. I think it looks a little bit like Stonecutters Island. There are lots of boats and ships in the harbour. Some of the humans on them wave as we pass.

I look up at all the white buildings on the harbour. Some of the men on the ship are lined up too, standing straight and excited to be getting off. Then I give myself a good old wash; I lick and clean every leg and my face. I want to be all ready for this new place, even if it might be a bit scary. I look up and see George with Peggy by his side.

'I'm a bit scared about this,' I say to Peggy as she comes up to me. 'A new place. We'll be all right though, won't we?'

'Oh, I'm not coming,' Peggy replies. 'I'm getting a bit too old for all that walking around. I think I'll just stay here and, you know, eat and sleep.'

My whiskers droop a little. That's a shame. I want my feeling of being brave to be bigger than my feeling of fear. And that would only happen if I get off the ship and go and explore with Peggy.

'Hey ho, Simon,' George says and lifts me up. 'Some of the lads are going to buy some food and have a bit of a drink up. D'you want to come too? Wiggle out of my arms if you don't.'

I just lie there in his arms. If I'm with George then I'll be safe.

Suddenly the Captain shouts and I jump.

'Attention!' The men all stamp their feet together — how silly, I wonder how they planned that trick without talking to each other — and go quiet.

'Crew,' the Captain barks. 'Back on board in six hours. Dismissed!' The men all run down the long tongue, talking and laughing. I feel as if I'm surrounded by good and happy. Once we step onto the dock, George puts me down on the ground. My legs are all wibbly wobbly as if I'm still on the ship.

'I think we'll go this way,' he says and heads off away from the dock. I run through many humans' legs to keep up with him, trying to look at all the stalls selling goodies as I do. When we turn into a street though it all changes. There are lots of pretty trees that make it cooler, but there's some water running next to the street. It's very dirty and very smelly indeed.

'Ah, those must be storm drains,' George says, picking me up again. 'I've heard of those.'

We come to a little shop and he makes me stay outside and wait. I look up and see lots of clothes on bamboo poles hanging out of windows. They stretch all across the alley, high up.

As I look back up at the clothes, I can see some... I don't know what they are... swinging about. One of them pulls some washing down as it climbs down the walls, swinging and jumping. They look like tiny furry children, not quite human. I can hear noise, not quite talking, more like lots of birds all tweeting at once. They're getting closer.

I wish George would come out. My fur stands on end and my nose twitches. I want to run into the shop, but George said I couldn't go in. Now my whiskers and tail are standing straight out too.

They're coming closer now; they've dropped onto the ground. One of them has seen me and shows me its teeth. This isn't good. They come over and circle me. They move more slowly and I can hear them sniff and see their noses move. I don't like this at all. I start to shake, my heart thumps and I can smell them coming towards me.

One of them tries to grab me. I jump out of its way and try to scamper through them, but another of them catches me by my fur. I yelp as its nails dig into my back. It shakes me and hugs me close to its chest. Suddenly, they all set off running through the alley, the little monster pressing me tight against it. Some humans point and laugh at us, but I know this isn't funny.

We turn into a big street. Bicycles and cars whizz past us. I can feel the hurt of the monster's hands on me, its nails digging into my back. My heart's pounding and there's a noise in my ears. I let out a squeal. Where's George? I want George. Or JoJo. I should never have left Stonecutters Island. I shouldn't have left the ship. I should have stayed on there where it was safe. What use is it being brave?

I can feel myself going up as we climb one of the trees; up, up. Human heads and the top of cars are below us. I've not been this high before and I don't like it. This isn't like flying. They're all around me. I'm thrown to another one. He catches me and strokes me hard. Too hard. These are not friends.

I give my best hiss, feel my fur stand on end and my tail stick straight out, but one of the monsters just grabs it. What are they going to do to me? Are they going to eat me? Where's George?

I'm trapped like the rats back on the ship, but I haven't done anything bad. I don't know what these monsters are saying. They just make scary noises. I don't like it here.

Suddenly we run down the tree. We get to the bottom and run back to the road. Where are we going? What are they going to do to me? I've never been more frightened. Ever.

As we run across the road I hear a shout over the noise of the cars. I see the big wheel of a car going round and round, moving fast before — bang! I feel it. We're not running. We roll over and over in the road. The car's hit the monster so it lets go of me. Quick! I jump to my feet, spy the other side of the road and run and run, in between the wheels of the cars and the bicycles. I look over, but nothing's coming after me.

I keep running and running, faster than I've ever run. I run round a corner, under a fence, before turning another corner and finding a wall. Phew. I'm shaking and my whole body is thumping. I'm very sore on my back. I crawl behind the wall and hide there, panting, thinking, panting.

I'm lost. I'm thirsty. I'm scared. I don't know what to do or where to go.

18/ It's magic

I lie and wait, hidden away from the road and away from the monsters. Perhaps if I walk slowly and follow my nose I might be able to find George again? Or the smell of the storm drain might help me?

Very slowly, I stand up and sniff. I can't smell anything I know, but I have to walk and keep walking. I go down the street, looking up and around all the time to see if the monsters are still around. The sun's hot on my back, making it really sore.

I walk and walk until I get to a big white building. I scamper over to a patch of grass in front of the building. I come to a tree, look up to see if there are any monsters in it, find a nice bit of shade and sit down underneath it. My back hurts, but it feels good to be out of the hot sun, to smell the grass and be away from everything and everyone. Almost everyone.

I think of JoJo. What would *he* do? I think of the place where I'm from. Do I wish I was back there? I don't know. I don't know if I would like to be there if JoJo wasn't. I think I'd like to just be on the ship. With Peggy and the Captain, with George and the others. On the ship I have my job and my friends. I have my games that I play with the Captain and with the other men, the die and the cold things I can't see. Here, I don't have anything and it's scary. I start to cry.

Then I start to yowl. I haven't made this noise before. I close my eyes and wish I wasn't here. I try to pretend the grass underneath my feet is the road in the port back home or the cold, hard floor on the ship that Peggy and I make the 'clack, clack' sound on. But it doesn't work. I know where I am. I'm here, all alone, with no one to snuggle up to or play with.

If I lie here and think then maybe I'll have a picture and I'll know what to do. I think and think, but a picture doesn't come. I look over at the building and, as I do, I think I see a wobbly shape I know sniffing around. Wait a minute, I know that shape! Of course I do. It's Peggy! Dear old, wobbly, lovely, always hungry Peggy! Now I see she is with Ginger and Atkins. I jump up and run, run, fast, fast, fast across the garden and almost leap onto her back.

'JoJo! JoJo! You're here!' I'm so happy, for a moment I even forget who she is.

'Why, yes.' She licks my face. I squeeze under her belly and come out the other side. 'When the chaps told me about this Raffles Hotel, I thought I must come and take a look. It's awfully grand isn't it? Exactly the kind of place I'd like to live in. And this beautiful garden. Heavens! It's just like mine was back home.'

Peggy stands back and takes a good look at me.

'Gosh, you look awful.'

Ginger strokes me. 'Thought you were with George? Oh crumbs, look at your back.'

But I don't care about my back. I don't even care if this place is grand or not. I just know that I feel safe and I don't want another adventure again. Not for a long while, thank you very much.

I tell Peggy everything that's happened as we lie on the grass. She doesn't know what the monsters were and at first she doesn't believe me. She does when I show her the marks on my back though.

'Battle scars,' she remarks. I don't know what she means. She must mean my back.

When it becomes darker, we go with Ginger and I make sure he picks me up and I stay in his arms all the time. The next best thing to George. He tells me and Peggy about everything we see as we walk past and as we sit down on some wooden stools.

I watch a man who's making some food for Ginger and Atkins. Ginger tells me what the man's doing. He points out the charcoal, a burner, a grill and some skewers. The cooking man stabs the meat with the skewers and puts them on the grill part. They spit and sizzle as if they're not happy to be cooked. The yummy smell soon gets into my nose and goes all the way down to my tail. It's called satay and, when it's cold enough for me to eat, I try it. It's the most yummy food I've had, apart from the food the Captain gave me of course. Maybe the monsters thought I was made out of satay?

When we've eaten, it's getting dark. The lights of the cars are like eyes and there are lamps everywhere, on the stalls and in the shops. I can still smell the storm drains a little bit, but I can smell the food being cooked all around even more. And I look to see if there are any monsters around. No, there are not. Phew!

We stop to watch some men who have cloth round their heads. One of the men has a huge snake around his neck. It hisses. I don't like it and cling to Ginger even more. But another of the men is moving cups around, which I do like. He hides something under one cup, moves them around and when he lifts the cup up, the thing hidden under it has gone. The brown men with cloth around their heads are called gulli gulli men and Ginger says they're magic.

'What's magic?' I whisper to Peggy.

'Magic is something which can't be explained,' she beams. 'Sometimes it is wonderful and sometimes it can be scary.'

Yes, I think. The ship. Here. All of it is magic...

19/ Full moon

On the ship I feel more happy than sad, but I sometimes feel funny. I speak to Peggy about it, but she doesn't really know what I mean. Sometimes I almost feel as if we're as close as a brother and a girl-brother and then other times I think she doesn't understand me at all.

'We're like chalk and cheese, dear Simon,' she gives a little chuckle when I tell her sometimes I feel funny. That just makes me even more confused.

We've just finished dropping titbits up on the stern. 'Aren't you getting frightfully bored with this, dear heart?' Peggy asks, as I sit down and wash myself. 'I never thought I would end my days as a slave to some rotten rat.'

A slave? End of days? But it isn't the end of the day. It still has to get hotter and colder and then night time.

'What d'you mean?'

'The Captain asked you to kill the rats, the filthy things, and instead here I am running around after them like... like an old maid.'

She looks a bit cross.

'Can't you, you know...? Don't you have it in you?'

I don't know what she means, but I know I must be doing something to make Peggy unhappy. Or not be doing something. She hasn't spoken to me like this before.

'I'm sorry,' she says finally and goes to give me a lick. 'I'm feeling rather unusual at the moment. I think I'll go back to my box and have a nice little snooze.'

Oh dear. I don't want Peggy to be all sad and not move around either. Maybe I should do something. Maybe I should try, really try...

That night, I go up onto the bow, breathe in and look out. I can see stars and can just about make out a cloud. Except for a light coming from the bridge, the rest of the ship is completely dark. Good, I like it when it's dark. I can see, see as well as a, well, as a me. I breathe out. Can I do this? I really want to be brave.

79

I pad down the port side, over… that, under… this, down the stairs into the doorway and through… here. I lift my head a little and give a little sniff. My whiskers are all stood on end. Another sniff. What was that? Oh, nothing, I just caught a whiff of some of the food we ate before. Quite nice it was too. I hide behind a bag of flour. Maybe I'll see a rat, maybe I won't.

I stretch my front legs out and my claws. Am I ready for this? I wait.

I smell something before I see it. A smell almost like the storm drains back in Singapore, but not nearly as bad. Not very nice though either. It smells of… it smells like. Yes! I smell a rat. A pink nose, long whiskers and pink feet run across a shelf just above my head. So they do still come in here! Greedy rats.

The rat jumps down from the shelf and onto the floor. It scampers across, stops and gives a little sniff. Maybe it can smell me too? It comes over right near me and the bag of flour. I get ready to pounce. My back legs are shaking, but I'm ready, ready to spring and to jump and to catch the rat. To dig my claws into its back just like the monster did with me. I stretch my front paws again, give my nose and whiskers a little twitch and, and…

I can't do it. My legs don't seem to want to jump. I look down and stare at my paws. Is this what Peggy means? That there's something in me that I don't have? Yes, there is something, it's a something that doesn't want to make things stop. When I get my funny, new feeling I sometimes want to jump high up into the air or at monsters chasing me, but I don't want to be Chairman. I want to be me.

I creep back outside, up the stairs and onto the deck. One star is winking, blinking at me more than the others. I look at it and look at it.

'Be careful what you wish for,' a voice behind me says. It's George, rubbing his eyes. 'I woke up and wondered where you were. Thought you might be in with the Captain.'

No. I've been somewhere else. Not doing my job properly. I give a little mew.

'Ah, you sound sad. Come here.' And he lifts me up and gives me a cuddle.

We sit down on the deck. I look up at him and then past him. The cloud isn't there anymore but the big, round thing I've seen before, but don't know the name of, is.

'Can you see it, Simon?' George whispers. Why's he whispering? There's no one else here. 'I love the moon, I do.'

Ah, so that's what it's called. The moon. What a lovely name for a lovely thing. I know I don't see it all the time. Sometimes I forget to look up, but sometimes it's not there. Other times it's high up and small, or low down and big. Sometimes it's as if a part of it has been eaten. I wonder why that is. If George can see it though and knows it has a name, then at least that must mean it's real, even if it's not there all the time. Maybe it's magic. The wonderful kind.

'You know, when I was very small,' George says, 'Somebody said to me the moon was made of cheese and I believed it almost until the day I joined the navy.' He gives a little laugh.

Cheese. That was what Peggy said she was, or maybe I was. Does that mean the moon is full of me's? Or dogs?

'How do we know it's not made of cheese anyway?' George continues. 'Nobody has ever been there. I suspect they never will either.'

I give him a look.

'You know, sometimes I think you can understand every word I say.' He rubs me between my ears. 'I'll let you into a secret. When I get lonely and miss home, I come up out here on deck and I look at the moon. I wonder if everyone I know back home can see it the same as me. Are they looking at it and thinking about me?'

He blinks, strokes me again and I purr. George stands up and makes for the stairs. I give a little wiggle and stretch my back legs out.

'Don't you want to go back in, Simon?' He looks at me.

No, I don't. I want to think about the moon and cheese. I want to think about if I'm good or bad because I didn't jump on the rat.

'OK.' He sets me down and disappears down the stairs.

I know I should make the rats stop. I should, I should. Peggy said a rat cannot be reasoned with and she must be right. Mao Tse Tung said they wouldn't go into the galley and help themselves and he was wrong. I don't know what to do. If we keep on giving them

81

food then Peggy will be unhappy, but if we stop giving them food they might just go into the galley more and more. If they do that then the men might all get poorly. I need to learn to be brave.

20/ What to do

I hear a noise coming from the bridge. It's a horrible, moaning, groaning sound. I think it may be the monsters again, but I know none of them came onto the ship. I checked. What shall I do? I decide to scamper up, up the stairs, go up to the bridge and see.

I run up and in. Lying on the floor is the Captain. He doesn't see me, but he makes a horrible noise. I circle round and round, sniffing him. He doesn't smell very nice. I tug his arm a little, but he just moves it away. I run back out, down the stairs, along the ship and into the lower deck. I jump right up onto George, put my face up to his and lick his nose. He stirs a little, so I lick it and lick it again. Then I claw him and mew.

His eyes open.

'What's wrong, Simon. What's the matter?'

I jump off him, turn and look back at him.

He swings his legs off the bed and follows me outside. I run, run, up, up to the bridge.

'Oh, my gosh,' he says and kneels down next to the Captain. 'Sir, sir. Are you all right?' George puts one hand behind the Captain's head and opens the Captain's eyes with the other. The Captain makes a horrible, growling sound.

'Sir, can you hear me?' George gives the Captain a little smack across his face. I'm sure that's not a very nice thing to do. The Captain opens his eyes and stops growling.

'Uh, huh. Feel sick,' he says. 'Water.'

George rushes off and I run over and rub against the Captain's hand. 'Ah, there you are. Good boy. Fine boy. Aah. Urgh,' and he strokes me a bit too hard. I can feel his hand all hot and wet.

George comes back with a jug of water. Does he want me to play with the things I can't see?

'That's right, Simon. You let the Captain stroke you. Make sure he doesn't fall asleep. I'm just going to cool him down.' He feels around, finds what looks like a little white flag in his pocket, dips it into the jug and dabs the Captain's face with it. George disappears again before coming back with a glass.

'Found this in his cabin.' He gives it a little shake and pours some water in from the jug.

'Here, sir. Drink this.' George tips the Captain's head forward. The Captain manages to take a sip of the drink George is holding up to his lips.

'I think it's just a fever you've got, sir. When we get back into Hong Kong, we'll get a doctor to check you out.'

Hong Kong! That's where I'm from. Are we going back there? I wonder if it'll still look the same. Or feel the same or smell the same. I know it won't *be* the same because of one thing of course. Will I even want to get off the ship when we get there?

George is still dabbing the Captain's face and making him drink. He looks a bit more awake now and a bit less scary.

'Where am I?' he asks.

'You're on the bridge, sir. You must have wandered out of your cabin.' George tells him.

'Good heavens. Surely not, no. D'you think you and Monty here can get me back into my cabin?'

'Aye, sir,' and George manages to lift him up and half drag him back into his cabin and place him back onto his bed. The Captain goes back to sleep even more quickly than Peggy. But at least he doesn't parp.

'Good job we heard him, eh, Simon?' George turns to me. 'He might have tried to set sail when we were still anchored down.'

That must mean trying to move after being stopped. I know how not possible that is.

'Come on,' George says. 'I think he'll be all right now. I think you should stay with me for what's left of this night.'

We leave the Captain and his being ill, step out of his cabin, walk out on deck, under the moon and back into the lower deck.

It still smells. Of cheese but maybe not chalk. Not that I know what that is. I'll have to ask Peggy what she meant by that when she wakes up. But for now, I'll just try and cover my nose with my paw.

21/ Begging bowl

Forwards, forwards into Hong Kong harbour. Before, it was my bottom waving goodbye, now it's my head saying hello.

The rats are still on the ship, the rats I know I must get rid of. I told Peggy about going to the galley and what happened, but she just shook her head. 'I don't want to say I told you so, Simon, but yes, well, I told you so.'

So, I need to come up with a good plan or be braver than I've ever been before. The Captain's still poorly too. He has red blotches all over his body and lots of the other men are ill as well. The rats must be doing something to them. I'm not poorly though. I just feel — what does Peggy say? — 'unusual' sometimes, although her unusual is different to mine. She just wants to sleep a lot. I want to pounce and scratch and jump.

I can see where I used to play on my jetty. My nose twitches at the thought of going back there. The place where I used to wait for the humans to come back in their boats and throw me some fish. Will they say hello to me if I go back?

I'd like to get off and have a sniff around again. I'm not scared of doing that in a place I know. A place where I'm from. Was from. Well, maybe a little bit scared. So long as I don't go up to the hill then I think I'll be OK. Or maybe if I just stayed close to George or Peggy then nothing or nobody could get me. Yes, that's what I'll do. Here comes George now.

'You look lost,' he smiles.

Of course I'm not lost. I know exactly where I am!

'Weston says we just need to get the men sorted out and then we'll be off back to Malaya. Bet you know the way there yourself now, eh?'

It's out through there, into the blue, and turn port, not starboard.

'Bet you can't wait to get back to your own place either?' he laughs.

As long as you come with me. How I wish I could tell him.

The ship's docked now and some sailors are moving the big tongue. Straight away, a man comes on, carrying a bag and nodding his head a lot as Weston speaks with him.

Peggy appears, her tail between her legs and her tongue hanging out.

'That's a doctor,' Peggy explains. 'To check on the ill sailors and make them better.'

'D'you want to come and see where I'm from?' I say. She's moved away from me to sit in some shade, away from the bright light and the hot sun beating down on the deck.

'Oh, no. It's far too hot for me.'

'Please, Peggy,' I mew. 'I want you to see.' I don't really want to tell her I'm just a little bit scared as well.

'Weeell. I could come I suppose. Will there be any food?'

I nod. I'm not sure where though.

'And drink?' Her tongue hangs out even more.

'Yes, I'm sure we'll find something to drink as well.'

'All right then.' She stands up, her belly wobbling. 'Lead the way.'

I shoot across the deck and scamper down the tongue, get to the bottom and wait for Peggy. She trots down, slipping a little as she does so. 'Whoops. Butterfeet.'

'Come on. This way, this way,' I say to her. It feels good to have my paws back on a place I know.

I run, run down the dock, then slow down as I realise Peggy hasn't caught up with me. She's sniffing everything as she walks along. Come on, hurry *up,* I think. Many human legs rush past as I wait for Peggy. I'd forgotten how busy it was here.

Peggy finally catches up with me, her tongue hanging out. 'I need a drink. Where d'you recommend?'

We sit outside a shop for a while, but it's no use, no one wants to stop and feed us.

'Aw. Hmm.' Peggy's ears droop. 'We really must do something about this, Simon. Here, let's go this way.'

What? What's this? Now she's showing *me* around. We turn down an alley, one that I know of course, but I've not been down since I was a very small me. I know we aren't near the green hill though, so no chance of bumping into you-know-who.

We get to a big shop. I can see lots of jars and tins piled up inside. Peggy stands back and looks up at the front of the shop.

'Ah, this is the place,' she turns to me and smiles. 'Follow me, dear Simon and do exactly as I do.'

She trots inside and sits across the doorway. I sit next to her, right near her bottom. Then decide to move to one side, just in case. We look up and see the owner standing behind the counter, talking to another human. She smiles at Peggy and Peggy makes her tail wag, before letting her tongue fall out and giving a little whimper. I stare at her and notice she has made her eyes go very big too. Bigger than I've ever seen her do.

I give a little mew and try to make my eyes do the same as hers, but I can't do it.

'Make another noise,' Peggy whispers to me, so I mew again, like I did when I was trying to get JoJo to play with me.

The owner calls to us. 'OK, OK, I see you. And you brought friend with you too.' Peggy moves her tail and hits the floor with it. Thump, thump, thump. The owner comes over to us and bends down.

'Where you been?' She rubs Peggy's head. 'When you go to live here? You want drink?' Peggy wags her tail even more and I stand and rub myself against the owner's legs. Round and round I go, my tail sticking straight up. The owner laughs and rubs my head as well.

The owner disappears and comes back with two bowls, a red one and another one; I'm not sure what colour it is. She puts one in front of me and the other in front of Peggy. We both stick our heads in the bowls at the same time; lap, lap, lap. Peggy looks at me mid lap and smiles.

We soon drink it all. It was just water, but I forget how lovely it is when you're very thirsty. Peggy then stands up, moves away from the bowl and, with difficulty, rolls over on her back. Her pink belly flops to one side as she tries to stick her legs up into the air. It doesn't really look very nice, but it must do what Peggy wants it to do because the owner's returned with two more bowls, this time with meaty food in. Again she puts one in front of me and gives the other to Peggy. I smell a familiar smell, put my head right up close to the bowl she's given me and have a taste.

Oh my gosh, it's the same as the food the Captain gave me. Whiskers. I still think it's a silly name, but it's still the most yummy food ever. I wonder if the owner has given Peggy the same as me. I try to push her big head out of the way of the bowl so I can have a little sniff. It doesn't smell the same. She's so busy eating that she actually gives me a little growl. She must have forgotten it's me.

I chew and eat and swallow. Chew, eat, swallow. Peggy has already eaten hers and puts her head into my bowl to try to eat some of mine. I bat her with my paw. Eh! Get away! I eat faster. I even feel a bit sick, but I don't care. There. All gone. I lick all around the bowl and finally rest my back legs by having a nice sit down.

Peggy's smiling again. 'Yum. Yum. Right, what's for pudding?'

The owner picks up our two empty bowls. 'You both very hungry. You not get fed where you live? Dear, dear.'

She rubs our heads and I try to give her my best smile. Peggy licks her hand.

We trot out of the shop.

'That place is called—' I start to say to Peggy.

'Yes. Lane Crawford. I know,' she answers.

'But how did you know?' Is she magic?

'We dogs know these things. Besides, I've been there before. Lots of times. Right, time for a nice little lie down, I think,' and she yawns. And then burps.

'Let me show you where I used to live and play,' I tell her. 'This way.'

'Oh, I'm far too tired for that now. I think I may just head back to the ship and have a lovely snooze,' she answers.

'Come on, Peggy. Please.'

'Really, Simon, I'm sure it's lovely, but I need a nice sleep on the ship,' she pants.

'OK then.' I feel a bit sad as she trots off. I watch her bottom and tail disappear amongst all the humans.

I skip over some ropes and round a cart. I keep hoping Chairman won't appear. I reach my favourite place where I used to lie, not far from the harbour. It feels strange to be back here. A place I thought I'd never leave and then thought I'd never see again. I feel happy that I've been brave to come here, but also sad that JoJo will never be here again. Funny to be feeling all sorts of different things at the same time.

What's the word? Opposite. Oh yes, I remember Peggy telling me when I asked her about the chalk and the cheese. That's how I feel. I feel opposite. And full.

I yawn, then I have a little stretch and I smile. It's quite windy. All I can smell is the salty air. It's nice to be here, but it'll be nicer to get back on the ship too.

I hear a gruff voice behind me.

'What are *you* doing here?'

22/ The best a cat can get

My whiskers stick straight out. My nose twitches, sniffing the air. I move my head slowly, my body hunched. Am I ready to spring out of the way, or to leap forward and scratch if I need to? I turn, shaking, waiting to see the large, bad, grey me with one staring green eye… who isn't there.

Instead, I'm greeted by a jumping-around-trying-to-leap-onto-his-shadow-oh-my-gosh-it's-so-good-to-see-him… Uboat.

'Hello, Uboat!' I leap on him. 'You wouldn't believe where I've been. I've been on a ship and met a dog and been chased by monsters in Singapore. I went there but not Malaya. I have to chase after rats… '

'All right, slow down,' he laughs.

Then I look past him. There, standing at the top of the steps, I spy a lovely white fur coat. As it runs down the steps towards me and Uboat, I smell a scent that gets right up my nose and makes my eyes and head spin.

It's Lilette, looking even lovelier than before. Lilette, the only other nice me I know in the place where I'm from — *was* from — is here, is here now. My head's spinning.

I wait for my head and the pictures to clear and breathe out.

'Hi, Lilette,' I say to her as she gives both of us a quick sniff. 'Hello,' she replies. 'I'm not sure I ever knew your name.'

'It's Simon,' I reply. I still feel a bit shy around her, especially when I tell her my name. Even Uboat gives me a funny look when I tell her. This is the first time I've ever said hello to her and she's said hello back. I hope I don't sound as silly as I think I do.

'I haven't seen you for a long time. Where have you been?' she smiles.

I tell Uboat and Lilette all about Chairman and JoJo and George.

'Poor JoJo,' mews Uboat and Lilette looks sad too.

I tell them about the Amethyst and Peggy and the rats. About McCunnell and the Captain. I make myself sound brave when I get to the scary parts, but I'm sure Uboat can tell I'm pretending.

'So that's where you've been,' Uboat says, giving me a lick. 'I told you that ships were fun.'

'Most of the time.' I give him a nudge with my paw.

'And what have you been doing?' I ask her. 'Where's Chairman?'

Lilette tells me about the places where she plays. About a nice man and woman who give her food, so she goes there every day. 'I haven't seen Chairman though. I think he may have gone,' she says. I wonder if she means really gone, or just not here anymore.

Then it's Uboat's turn to tell me about where he's been. About a big storm and having to sail somewhere so his ship could be mended. 'It's much more exciting having adventures than just listening to them, isn't it?'

He's right. I used to love listening to his stories, but it's a lot more fun now I can understand more of the things he talks about and I have tales of my own. I have tales and a tail. How funny.

We all sit there for a long time, enjoying the feel of the hot sun, being together and knowing that Chairman is nowhere to be seen or found.

'D'you want to go and get some food?' Lilette asks us both.

'No, thank you,' Uboat replies. 'My ship will be going soon and I just know there'll be some lovely food on there waiting for me.' We rub noses and he scampers up the steps, down, round and away.

Lilette gets up and moves a little closer to me. I feel all warm and shy.

'What about the nice man and woman,' I say to her. 'Could we go and visit them?'

'What a great idea,' she smiles. 'Let's go.'

And so we spring together up the steps, across the street, down one of the alleys and run up, up away from the harbour. We get to a dusty track and walk down it. Some of the dust has covered Lilette's lovely white fur on her belly.

We reach a house with a fence outside. Lilette squeezes through a gap and I follow her. I don't think Peggy would have been able to squeeze through. It's very tiny. Even I only just about make it.

She mews as we reach a door. It opens and a human looks down at us both.

'Hello, hello, where have you been?' the woman says. 'And my, who's this?'

I lift my tail up and let myself be stroked by her. She's wearing a very pretty dress and smells even more like flowers than flowers do.

Lilette and I both follow the woman. We pad across a tiled floor and the woman places two bowls in front of us and fills them with food. It's nice, but not as nice as the magic food in the tin from the Captain or from the shop owner. I eat it anyway!

When we've finished eating and the woman has given us some water, a man comes in. He picks Lilette up. I think she might scratch him, but she doesn't. She lets him take her through to another room. I follow and watch. He has a tiny broom with him. Is he going to try and make Lilette and me do some cleaning?!

Ah, I see now. He strokes Lilette's back with it and brushes and brushes and brushes her so she's very clean. Her fur all fluffs up as he brushes the dust away from her belly. He even cleans her paws with a cloth. I think I would sneeze and pull them away if someone tried to do that to me.

At last he stops brushing Lilette. She drops down from his knees. She looks lovely.

'What about you?' the man says to me. 'D'want to have a nice brush too?'

I stand and stare at him. I don't really want to go over.

'Go on,' Lilette nods. 'Haven't you ever been brushed before?'

No, I haven't! I like to clean myself. I don't know if I would like a human to do it for me. Do humans clean each other, I wonder.

The woman looks down at me and smiles. 'It does feel marvellous.' Perhaps humans *do* brush each other then. How odd.

And so I creep slowly over to the man. He pats his knee. I look over at Lilette again and then jump up on him. I can feel his hand on my back and then it feels as if I'm trying to run under something because it scrapes all along. Ouch. It hurts. He must brush over my... scattle bars, as Peggy calls them, because it stings. Then the man must see them because he says, 'Oh, you poor little thing. Who did that to you?'

He stops brushing my back and does my belly instead. Then he brushes my front and back legs. Sometimes, he has to brush quite hard and pull. 'You've got a few clumps in here,' he says. 'Have you fallen in the sea?' I can see some of my hairs in the brush. I hope he doesn't brush me away completely!

He gives my head a little brush and I can feel all my fur spring up. I think I prefer cleaning myself to be honest, but I want to look brave in front of Lilette.

'There you go,' the man says after a while and puts the brush down. 'Looks like you've been in the wars a little, but you're all shipshape now.'

I might not know what the wars are, but I know I'm not the shape of a ship!

I feel all light. All clean and fluffy. I hope I look as good as Lilette.

We trot through the house until we reach a door. Lilette mews. The woman's followed us. 'So, you want to go back outside? OK then,' and she opens the door and lets us both out.

We run across the garden, squeeze through the gap and out along the track. It's darker now, but the stars are out. I can see all the ships.

'That's mine,' I say to Lilette, pointing out the Amethyst. 'That's where I live.'

'Tell me another story,' she whispers and nuzzles up to me. I feel, what was it Peggy said? As if I'd been eating butterflies? No, I feel much better than that.

And so I tell her about playing with the die. About the brown drink and the Captain who is ill. More stories about the rats and what I must do to them.

'You're very brave,' she says to me. 'I haven't been anywhere except this place.'

'But you like it here though, don't you?' I ask her.

'Oh yes. I like the humans who feed me and look after me. I don't know if I'd want to be anywhere else.'

That's what I used to think, I think.

We sit there and carry on looking down at the ships below and at the stars up above. There are more stars now, twinkling down.

My head spins as I listen to her. Her scent is all around me. It seems to get stronger. Then she leaps up and runs back down the track fast, fast. Spinning around and jumping behind trees. I spring over her, around her. We laugh and smile a lot. I wish we'd played together a lot more before George had found me. I wish I'd been braver. We have so much fun and I feel a much, much happier cat after being with her.

23/ Sad but happy

It's almost bright when I get back to the Amethyst. On the way back I come across a small, stopped bird, so I pick it up, thinking that George might quite like it. Gurns sees me as I trot along the dock. He kindly puts the tongue out so I can run back up.

I skip along, looking for Peggy, but there's no sign of her. I wish I could ask Gurns where she is.

I think I see a dark shape run quickly past. Not Peggy. Too small and much too fast. I try to follow the shape to see where it ran off to, but it's gone now. I'm just about to go and find George when I hear a small whimper. I run right to the back of the engine room. There, hiding behind a pipe, is Peggy. She looks sadder than I've ever seen anyone. Even sadder than when George's eyes are wet. I drop the bird.

'Peggy, Peggy. It's me. What's wrong?'

Her head is buried in her paws and her ears are right, right down. She moves a paw away from her face and stares up at me. Big, brown, wet, sad eyes.

'Oh, Simon.'

'What? What is it?' I want to know. I squeeze in next to her and she shuffles over a little. 'Lots of the sailors are ill,' she sniffles. 'Some of them have to sleep away from the others for a while. But some of them have been taken away. And the Captain... he's gone.'

Gone. Not that word again.

'The Doctor came and said the Captain should go with him. So they've both left. He won't be coming back,' and Peggy cries again.

So, not gone, but not on this ship anymore. It's still very sad though. Who will be the Captain now? Who will play the die game with me? Whose hat will I sleep in?

'He rescued me and looked after me. Who will do that now?' she whimpers.

'Oh, Peggy. You have me. We'll look after each other. The sailors will still feed us.'

She looks up. 'I wish I could've said goodbye. I wish I could've licked his hand. It was all very quick.'

I was happy before; now I feel sad again. Funny how things can change so quickly. I don't know what to do. Or what to say. What will make Peggy feel happier?

'What d'you need?' I say to her. 'D'you need a lick?' She nods her head and gives a little smile. I lick her wet nose. 'D'you need some food?' I ask her. Her smile is bigger, her head noddier. She looks at my bird.

'You're not having that,' I say to her. 'That's for George.'

I run out of the engine room, up the stairs, through the doorway, round and out onto the deck. I don't quite know where I'm going to get some food from, but I'll find some. Anything to make Peggy feel more like herself.

I scamper up to the bow. I'm just about to go up to the bridge when I spy Mao Tse Tung! Rats are running up the tongue one at a time. He squeaks something to them and they run off starboard. Here's another one. And another. They scurry right across the deck of the ship. *Our* ship.

I shrink back. Oh no! This is too bad. Peggy was right and I was wrong. We've been feeding them, helping them so they won't make my friends ill and now there are more and more of them coming on board. Mao Tse Tung must have told them how easy it is to live on this ship. To be fed by a cat and a dog instead of being chased by them. Chased and caught by *me*.

I feel the opposite of how I felt when I was with Lilette. I don't want the rats to see me. Not just yet. I don't want to be seen and I don't want to feel like this. I want to be a happy cat again. I want Peggy to be a happy dog too. How can I tell her what I've just seen? She will be sadder than ever. I find myself in the lower deck, squeeze through all the swinging beds and jump up on George.

'Where've you been?' he asks. 'I thought you were never going to come back. And what's that you've got?'

I mew and drop the bird on him.

100

'Er. Thanks.' George picks it off himself — I can tell he likes it — and drops it on the floor. He picks up a small bag next to his present. 'And I have something for you and Peggy. Well, from the Captain. Weston was helping him to pack. He put something in there for you too.'

George places the bag on his chest in front of me. I stick my nose in and it rustles a little. I can't smell anything. Wait! I can now. Something I know. George puts his hand in and brings out a small... it's the die. The Captain's die! He left it for me. George puts his hand in the bag again and pulls out a... what is it? It's an old chewed sock, with a bit on the top that looks like it has been ripped off.

Oh, I know what this is! I didn't understand what George and Conway were shouting to each other about socks but I *do* know this is an old, blue, smelly sock.

No, it isn't! It's got an ear. It must be Peggy's smelly old sock toy monkey. I might not know what a monkey is, but by the look of this one I really hope I do one day because they look cute and lovely. And I know this smell of course and I know exactly who it belongs to. What did I say about wanting to make Peggy happy again?

I leap off the bed and run, run, run back down to the engine room.

'Hey!' George calls after me.

24/ Good and bad

I'm on the mess deck with Peggy, her monkey and some of the sailors. We have a new Captain though. His name's Skinner. He's here because the other Captain was too poorly to carry on.

Peggy's lying under a table, chewing; the sailors are eating and I'm licking. I think that now might be the right moment to tell Peggy about the rats. Now is all we have, after all.

I peer out from behind my back leg.

'Peggy,' I call over to her, but she's too busy munching.

'Peggy,' I hiss again. She looks up, spit running from her mouth down onto her monkey's head. 'Mmm. What? What is it? Is it food time?' Both her ears prick up.

'No, but it's about the food. Sort of.'

The monkey's ear flops forward. So does one of Peggy's.

I pad over to her. 'Have you noticed we're taking more and more food up to the stern?' I ask her.

'Not sure,' she mumbles between chomps. 'But we've been doing a lot more walking. D'you want a chew?'

'No thanks. Well, I think... No, in fact I *know* Mao Tse Tung must have told some other rats about being fed all the time. There's... twenteen more rats than when I first came on board. Lots of them.'

'Are you sure, dear heart?' she answers.

'Yes. I think sometimes I can see them. Can't you smell them?' I look around, almost expecting some rats to run through the mess deck right there and then.

'Well, we'll just have to put a stop to them this time, won't we?' Peggy answers.

I know she's right. I wish I knew how to though.

Weston comes in with the Captain. 'Attention!' and all the sailors stop eating, stand up straight away and hit the side of their head with their starboard hand. Even I stand up. Peggy doesn't though; she just flops over to one side. The Captain sees me, but he doesn't smile at me like the other one used to.

'We've just had an order come over the wireless,' the Captain says, looking back at the sailors. 'We have to head down to Nanking.'

'Why, sir?' Atkins pipes up.

'I'm coming to that,' the Captain snaps, quite grumpily. 'Some of our boys on HMS Consort have run into some trouble. HMS London is on her way too. Consort has come under fire from some of the darned Chinese Communists and we can't have any of our ships being fired on. Weston will keep you informed,' and he walks out.

All the sailors start talking and raising their voices after the Captain walks out.

'Why are they being fired at?' George asks Weston.

'Don't know,' he answers.

'Will we get fired at by the Commies?'

'No, we darned won't,' Weston answers. 'We'll fly our white flag and the Union Jack and paint the Union Jack on the hull as well. That'll show them who we are.'

I hope he's right! I quite like the sound of this Nanking place. I wonder why it's called that. Maybe it's because a king lives there. Not long now until I find out, I suppose…

****

Later, I'm lying on top of George. I've just finished taking food up onto the stern with Peggy. It's much harder now because she doesn't want to let go of her toy monkey now she's found it again. Sometimes I even have to pull it off her and drop it into her box.

'No one will take it away from you again,' I mew at her. I know how she feels about her toy though. The only thing I really used to play with all the time was JoJo and I know how much I miss him; his shape, his smell, his ears.

'We reach Nanking in the morning then,' George says, rubbing my head. I purr and stretch my claws out.

'Ow. Don't do that,' he chuckles, moving them away. Then he looks a little scared and worried.

'I do hope everything will be OK,' and he touches one of the pictures next to his swinging bed.

I know things will be OK though. I can sense it. From being a scared little me hiding and George finding me, coming here on this ship, meeting Peggy, the very nice Captain and the not very nice McCunnell, almost getting thrown overboard, being chased by monsters in Singapore and playing with Lilette, my one life so far has been wonderfully exciting.

What did Peggy say? That there was good and bad in everyone, in everything. Since I came on board this ship there's been some bad, but there's been lots and lots of good as well. Everything is magic, Peggy's right. And I'm right as well; everything is good and will carry on being good.

25/ Peggy's story

'There I was in my box, with monkey by my side of course, when I was woken by the most beastly sound. Louder than if all the dogs in the world barked at the same time.

'I'm used to all the sailors shouting and running around — sometimes they even put their heads right into my box and shout, 'Peggy, Peggy,' — but this noise was truly horrible after someone shouted, 'Action stations!'

'And then — whoosh! And a boom! It nearly knocked me right out of my box, it did. I stepped out of it to see what all the fuss was for and was just about to walk out onto the deck when lots of legs came rushing past me. All I heard was, 'Over there! Look out!'

'What on earth is happening? I thought. 'Peggy! Get back!' I heard someone else shout. The air was quite smoky and I saw some of the men put Union Jacks over the side of the boat. I trotted round to the other side and just got to the bow when 'Kaboom!!'

'Oh, it was dreadful, it really was. Someone's attacking us, I thought. I haven't even had my breakfast yet.

'I decided to head up to the bridge — even though I know I'm not allowed in there. Then I heard more firing coming from the land I could just about make out and I saw a shell splash right across the bow. Let me tell you, I moved more quickly than I ever have before – faster even than when I was a puppy.

''Someone's firing at us,' I heard the Captain shout. Oh, my poor ears. I couldn't get away from the noise. I heard another whoosh and then it became very frightening because one side of the bridge just smashed in completely. Some of the men around me were flung over and fell right onto the deck. I was shaking all over, from my head right down to my tail.

'And then the smoke appeared. Gosh, it was terrible. Thick and black and really stinging my eyes and throat. Welburn was at the wheel, but it looked as if he'd been hurt too. As I watched, he slid to the floor, knocked the wheel and I felt the whole ship lurch.

'I managed to get away, but had to keep stepping over men and I really couldn't see much. I was grateful I couldn't see the land because that meant whoever was attacking us couldn't see me. I always thought I wanted to be a much bigger dog, but I was awfully thankful of my size at that moment.

'From my hiding place, I could see sailors trying to fire back at whoever was attacking us, but I don't think it was any use. Everything was flying everywhere. When was this ever going to end?

'Then the ship shook to a halt with a massive crunch. I thought we must have hit something, but we must have smashed into shallower waters. With no one at the wheel, there was no one to steer the ship, so it just drifted until it ran aground.

'Everyone was trying to escape from the smoke and the smell, but lots of the sailors were very poorly.

'We need to shut the engines down,' I heard Weston command. 'Did we manage to send the distress signal out?'

"Yes, one was sent. 'Under heavy fire. Am aground. Large number of casualties."

"Good.' Weston snapped. 'They'll be sending a ship up no doubt. Think HMS London is near the Yangtze River. Right, who's with me to get some of our men ashore?'

'Lots of men volunteered and started to pull on ropes on the side of the ship to lower one of the boats into the water.

"The rest of you, I hope you've got your water wings because you're going to have to swim for it,' Weston added.

'I stuck my head out through the railing and could just about see the water below. Some of the men stood up or crawled over to get in the boat, and others started to swim, even though a 'rat-a-tat' noise started up.

'When are they going to stop firing? I thought. There weren't many of us left on the ship now.

'I went back down to the lower decks, but it was horrid, with poorly sailors everywhere. Then, oh heavens above, I saw George sitting on the floor in the corner. He was rubbing his face and didn't seem to know where he was, so I wandered over and sat down next to him.

'He stroked my head and we sat there and watched what was going on. Then, very, very slowly, he stood up, using one hand to steady himself against the side of the ship. 'I need to make sure everyone's all right,' he said to me and he went to head out. I really didn't want to leave him, but I didn't want to go back out on deck either. I thought it may be best if I just followed him. So out we went.

'The whole ship was a mess. We moved very slowly, George kicking things out of the way to clear a path for me. We got to the bridge, or what was left of the bridge anyway. It was completely smashed to pieces. There's an awful lot of clearing up to be done, I thought when I saw all the mess. That's going to take an awfully long time.

'And as George and I picked our way through all the bits of ship, we got to the bow and there, when we looked down, lying underneath a whole heap of goodness knows what, my heart nearly jumped out of my throat, because that's when we found... you, Simon!'

26/ What next?

Something bad's happened and I feel bad. My ears are still screaming, as if all the monsters from Singapore are in my head, running around.

Peggy's panting. She's told me the story about what just happened. My head hurts. Everything hurts. One minute I was curled up, nice and warm, and about to have a little snooze and the next — bang! I remember some things, but not everything.

I see Peggy's face and then picture Chairman. Did I really see him? His glinting green eye? Why was someone shooting at us? Peggy said there's good and bad everywhere, in everyone. Where's the good now? Peggy tries to give me a lick, but it stings too much when she does. I just want to lie here, wherever here is.

'Where's George?' I croak, my throat dry and sore.

'He's looking after some of the others,' she answers. 'Oh, Simon, you look awful, if you don't mind my saying so.'

I try to blink, but it's very hard. Wherever I am smells horrible, but then I realise the smell's coming from me. I try to move my head, to peer round and look at my back. Maybe I could give myself a clean? Ouch. Ow. No, it hurts too much.

'Don't move,' Peggy says quietly. 'You're pretty poorly. The doctor had to take bits of metal out from you, you know, and even stitch you back together,' she shivers. 'They thought you were... you know... ' but she stops, and looks very sad.

Does she mean I nearly *stopped*?

'Are we still on the ship?' I ask her, looking around as best I can.

I try to lift my head to look, but I can't really make anything out. The smell of... burnt... seems to be coming from everywhere, not just from me. I try to close my eyes again.

'Hey, Simon,' I hear a voice. George. 'My, my,' and I feel the touch of his hand, but shrink back.

'Sorry. Oh, you poor thing. Your back. We thought we'd lost you, you know... '

No, I wasn't lost. I was just... not here for a while. Did I really come close to... what happened to JoJo? I hear the sound of feet running and someone bursting in.

'They've sent a rescue party! The HMS Consort.'

I hear a sailor mumble. 'Good, they can get us off this darned thing.'

'I'd best get upstairs,' George's voice. 'Peggy, d'you want to come too or stay here with Simon?'

I open my eyes and peer down at Peggy. She looks up at George. Then at me. Even though I'm hurting all over and can't really move, I want to see everything. I want to be there for George. I want to see the ship coming to rescue us. I whisper to Peggy, 'I want to see,' and try to sit up.

'Here, no moving for you just yet,' George orders. He wraps me in the blanket I'm lying on and very slowly, carefully, lifts me up.

We leave the horrible smell and the poor sailors in the room, go through a doorway and make our way up and out onto the deck. In the distance, I see a ship coming towards us, a bit like ours. I look up and see flashes of light coming from our ship. The HMS Consort flashes back. It's as if they're speaking, but without words.

Some of the sailors are waving their hands in the air. They're smiling, but they don't look happy either. George must see the Captain because I hear him shout, 'Sir,' and, for a moment, he takes one of his arms away from under me.

The Captain looks ill. Even more ill than the first one. He coughs and staggers as if his legs are as wibbly wobbly as mine. Suddenly he falls to his knees, right in front of us on the deck. I don't like this at all. I try to curl myself up into a small ball under George's arm. Peggy whimpers.

'Over here!' George calls to someone. 'Get him below deck.'

The Consort's getting closer. Not long now before we're all rescued and safe, even safer than here under George's arm. Peggy gives a little wag of her tail. I can see one, two, three flags on it as it

gets closer, the same as we have on here. Then I see even more —
one, two, three, five, four, six, seven. I've done it!

There's a 'crack, crack, crack' and I hear Peggy howl, 'No!
Not again!' and she runs off.

Whizz! Crack! Now I try and make myself really small.
George throws himself on the deck. I feel us falling forward and down.

I'm scared, scared, scared. We half crawl, half run right round
to the other side of the ship, away from the land where the huge bangs
are coming from, round to the other side. I see the Consort sailing right
up close to us, smoke coming from the top of it. The bangs stop as it
sails past us. Wait! Wait! What about rescue? George rescued me and
brought me on here, now they have come to rescue us to get us all off.
Why are they sailing past? Where are they going? Why haven't they
stopped?

The Consort sails away. George sighs and his eyes go wet.
'OK, let's get down below. See how everyone is,' George says and
we rush downstairs.

'I'm frightfully sorry for dashing off Simon,' Peggy says as
she sees us. 'I just couldn't face it all again. I don't know whether I'm
coming or going.' She looks very sorry for herself. 'I think I might
even have done my business up there. Not very considerate I know.' I
sneeze a little and George must think I want to get down because he
gently places me near Peggy. I nuzzle up next to her, glad of her
warmth.

'Are we stranded here?' I hear someone call out.

'Not for long!' Another voice. 'I'll get something working.
We'll get a signal out.'

I see McCunnell, all quiet and curled up on the floor. I walk
slowly over to where he's sitting. I lie next to him. He looks down,
but I don't know if he sees me. Then I feel his hand on my head. Soft…
gentle…

'We've sent a message out!' somebody suddenly shouts. 'We
got a message that HMS Black Swan and HMS London are on their
way.'

At that moment, I hear a rumble coming from underneath my paws. The engines! They're starting up. The ship grumbles into life. It creaks and rattles. Peggy trots over to me. We're moving!

'Shan't be long now,' Peggy mutters. Then we hear the sound of loud bangs again. 'Oh, I spoke too soon,' and she lets out a loud noise of her own. This is the first time I've wished I wasn't here.

I hear bang, bang, bang and feel us moving slowly, slowly. We must be moving away from the bangs. We haven't sunk. We've done it!

Slowly, Peggy lifts herself up. 'I think I may go and explore. Now it's, um, safer,' and off she trots, her tail between her legs. I think I know where she's going. She soon returns, carrying something in her mouth. I was right. She looks both happy and sad.

'I found these biscuits.' She tries to make her tail wag. I try to eat some, but my throat is still very dry and sore. I nibble. I cough. The sailors groan. Peggy eats all of her biscuit. And some of mine. We lie there. And wait.

Damage to HMS Amethyst
Photo from Lieutenant Commander Stewart Hett

Damage to HMS Amethyst
Photo from Lieutenant Commander Stewart Hett

27/ Time for work

I'm surrounded by unhappy. When we heard that the Black Swan and London were only a few miles away, all of the sailors smiled. Our ship had been refloated and we had managed to sail a bit further down the river to where it was safer. Peggy was excited at the picture of getting off the ship. I heard some of the injured sailors say they were looking forward to being able to go back to the places where they're from.

But the ships weren't able to rescue us in the end, not like how George had rescued me all that time ago.

After the ships didn't rescue us, a plane landed on the sea. How strange. I've seen them fly in the sky but not land on water. It looked like a big bird. The plane had a doctor on board. The plane didn't stay long though. As soon as it landed, the bangs all started up again and so it flew off pretty quickly. The doctor must be very brave to jump onto the ship while the Commies were firing!

A few days later, a small boat came with our new Captain. The boat took more injured sailors away, even though they didn't want to leave the ship; they all wanted to stay on here and help.

The new Captain's called Kerans. When he arrived on the ship, George carried me under his arm and we went with another sailor called Hett to say hello to him. George says Hett's an Officer, which means he's more important than the other sailors on board. Kerans spoke to George and Hett, but he didn't say hello to me.

I think he's very strict, even stricter than the other Captain, but George said the sailors need someone to take charge, to make us and the Amethyst shipshape again. I've heard that before. Now I know it means better and ready.

The sailors smiled when Kerans said someone called a journalist in Hong Kong had heard what was happening to us. The journalist told the world about it and now the whole world knows where we are, but can't do anything about it. How can one human tell the whole world something anyway?! That's a *lot* of telling. And how could a whole world even help us now?

117

The only other time the sailors were happy was when they were told of some of our friends who'd swum to the land when we first became stranded. They'd had to walk across land that had things in called mines which bang and explode if you stand on them. None of them had exploded though so all the sailors were OK. Phew!

Some who left the ship are now in a place called a hospital. Captain Skinner and some of the others died too. Ginger was one of the sailors who died. That made me very sad when George told Peggy and me.

And now we've been on here for a long, long time. I'm starting to feel better though. My back and head are still sore and my paws still hurt when I put them on the floor, but I can move around.

I think of the rats running around, eating all the sailors' food, and making them ill. I didn't used to think some creatures were better than others, but now I'm not so sure. If Peggy and I can be friends then why can't other creatures or humans be friends too?

But if one creature or human wants to get rid of another one then that means they're bad. It should be the bad ones, not the good ones, who go away, I think. If creatures or humans don't care, or want to cause hurt, then they need to be stopped. So that's why I need to stop the rats. It would be better for the sailors if the rats weren't on this ship. I have to kill them. I understand that now.

Mao Tse Tung must have told lots and lots of rats to come on board. I've even seen them nibbling the toes of the poor sailors down below. That's why Peggy was looking happy and sad when she came back with some biscuits when we didn't get rescued. She said she'd seen them running around too. I know what I need to do.

So, as the sailors and I slowly start to get better, I prowl round the ship. I know I can't run fast but, whenever I smell that I'm near a rat, I hide and I wait. After smelling them, I hear them, snuffling and scratching on the floor. Then I see one. A pink twitching nose. My ears twitch too. I crouch, my claws stretch straight out and then... I spring! Forward, my claws digging into its back, just like the scary monsters in Singapore did to me. But I'm doing this because I have to and because it's the right thing to do.

The first time I did it and caught a rat I very nearly felt sorry for it and I was going to let it go. But then I thought of Chairman and his one green eye, I thought of the sailors and how ill they look and I kept on biting and clawing until it stopped moving. I know I couldn't have done it a long time ago, but I can do it now. I do it to protect my friends and to do my job. Finally, I'm a cat who's got the rats!

I walk all around the ship, along the deck and down below. I sniff. I wait. I hunt. Then I clean myself. I sit or lie with the sailors and, when they're asleep at night time, I hunt again. One time Atkins showed one of the rats I had killed to some of the other sailors.

'Brilliant work,' Gurns said. 'Getting rid of the enemy for us. Keep it up.'

28/ One hundred and one sleeps

Sometimes, when I'm not doing my job, I sit with the sailors when they're listening to something called a radio. They all stand around a box and humans speak to them and there are lovely sounds like back home in the place where humans moved around and my bottom wanted to wiggle. I think it's magic.

The sailors don't use it very often though because it uses power but, when they do, it seems to make them smile. They listen to voices coming from very far away. George says it helps him and the others to think of home.

I try to comfort the sailors by lying next to them. I know I can't lick them and try to make them clean, but I can lie there and if they want to stroke me on my head then they can. Some of them want to and seem to like it when I go over, but others just want to be left alone.

Just like when I first met McCunnell and I could tell he didn't like me, I think I can tell which sailors want me to be with them and which ones don't. My whiskers twitch and tell me which ones to go and lie on, or next to. I still like to sleep on top of George though, so sometimes I sleep on him and other times I stay with the poorly sailors.

'Thanks, Simon,' some of them say. 'What would we do without you? Keeping us happy. Reminding us of home.'

George says we're rationing our food. It means not eating very much at all. There's not much food for anyone, not even for Peggy and me. Her belly doesn't wobble as much anymore.

I don't think Kerans likes me very much. He's always busy, or shouting. Sometimes he gets in a small boat, goes away and then comes back again. George says it's because he's going to meetings with some important Commies. Strange how he goes to see the people who wanted us all dead. He must be very brave. He always comes back though, but when he does he is *very* angry.

121

I don't understand what Kerans talks about, but he says the Commies won't let us be rescued. The Commies say they attacked us because we attacked them first, but I know that's not true or even real.

Peggy said we were just sailing down the Yangtze River to help the Consort when all the banging started. If Kerans says to the Commies that we fired first then they'll let us go, but he won't do that because that didn't happen. So, right now, it's more important to be true and real than to pretend, even though we might be able to sail away if Kerans said that.

I wonder if I would be true and real if I were him. If by pretending it meant I could be with Uboat again, or Lilette, then I think I might just pretend. I don't think I like this adventure anymore.

It's very hot now on the ship as well. My fur's too hot and, however often I lick myself, I can't cool down. I don't know where to put myself. Peggy doesn't either. I try to make her happy as well as the sailors. Sometimes she nuzzles me, but sometimes she tells me to go away.

George says he and the other sailors are happy to have me around though, which means they like it that I'm on this ship. What did the first Captain say to me all that time ago? That we all have a job to do, including me. Well, my job is to hunt the rats so, until we all get rescued, that's what I do now.

****

Peggy, me, George, Gurns and some of the other sailors are in the mess. I can tell by the smell of what they're drinking that it must be the brown stuff. Even though I don't like the smell of it, and certainly not the taste — George put some on his finger once and I had a lick, but it was horrible — it smells better than the ship smells now. While we've been waiting, the sailors often roll little papers and set fire to them. It's smoke that comes out, not fog. I know that now. I still don't like it though.

Kerans comes in.

'Any news, Captain?' Atkins asks, knocking back some of his drink.

'We're sending messages back home, but there's no movement I'm afraid. Still a darned cat and mouse game those Commies are playing,' Kerans answers, gruffly.

Cat and mouse? So where are the cats and where are the mouses? Maybe he means rats?

'Can't stay here forever though,' Kerans continues. 'And we don't have much fuel left. Any of that for me?' he asks, pointing at Atkins's drink.

Atkins pours him a glass.

'So what are we going to do?' Gurns asks.

'Leave it with me,' Kerans snaps. 'They brought me on here to get you boys out and, by gum, I will.' He drinks all his drink in one go. 'I'm working on a plan. You'll receive my orders soon enough. The early bird catches the worm and all that,' and he marches out.

Birds? Worms? I like Kerans talking about all these creatures, but I like the sound that he has a plan even more.

Simon, Peggy and the crew while the ship was trapped – July 1949
Photo from Lieutenant Commander Stewart Hett

29/ Have to be brave

I'm walking around the deck. I asked Peggy if she wanted to walk round with me, but she said she didn't. The hotter it is, the less she wants to move. The less we eat, the less she wants to move. I wish I could make her happier. Even though I'm very hungry, I still want to move around.

We've been on here for a *long* time now. Every time I see the moon, I want to remember how many times I've seen it and add it to all the other numbers, but sometimes the moon isn't there and sometimes I just forget.

I've done lots of purring and being stroked. I've killed lots of rats, but I know I still have a lot more to kill. I've sat on sailors' laps and slept next to them. There've been lots and lots of days and sleep and not so many biscuits or fun. But at least I've been getting better and the sailors have been too.

The bridge still looks hurt when I walk round it. The ship works though because we sailed away from the really scary place with the bangs to this part of the river, but I wonder how long the ship will be able to sail for. It doesn't look like it could get very far when I see all the broken parts.

Suddenly, I hear some snuffling. Maybe it's the rats! Oh no! There is a *huge* big shadow, right in the corner, bigger even than Mao Tse Tung. My legs go all wobbly and I have to plonk myself down. Shhhh!

I hear lots of sniffling and sneak a look. It's one of the sailors, sitting on a box with a bag beside it. 'Make it stop, make it stop,' he keeps groaning. He has his hands over his ears and is shaking his head as if he wants it to fall off. His shoulders shake up and down and his body's shaking too. Maybe he's cold.

I trot over to give him a cuddle. Maybe I'll make him feel better. But, as I get near, he lifts his head and... oh no... it's McCunnell!

'Oh, Simon,' he sniffs. 'Siiimooon.' He sounds like he's wailing, like I did after JoJo.

I edge closer. I'm not sure what to do. He hates me. But he looks so sad. More alone than I felt before George found me. Maybe McCunnell needs finding. I curl up beside him, but peep to see if he will slap me away.

His hand reaches out, strokes my head, my ears. Softly. Carefully. Gently he picks me up and cuddles me. I feel wet on my fur as he buries his face in me and whimpers. Poor McCunnell.

'Thank you, Simon,' he whispers, as he stands up and puts me on deck. 'Thank you.' And off he walks towards the bridge. I'm not sure what I did, but he seems happy.

Seeing McCunnell huddled on a box in the corner has given me another picture. I have to tell Peggy. I find her in the stowage, all curled up.

'Peggy. Peggy. Wake up.'

She doesn't move.

'Peggy.' I manage to jump right into the box and land on top of her.

'Grrr. Snuffle. Biscuits. What is it?' She wakes up and flicks her ears.

'I think it's time we got rid of the rats. Once and for all.'

'Can't it wait, dear?' She nuzzles me. 'I'm most awfully comfortable here.'

'No, no. We've got to do it now. The sailors don't have much food and what they have we need to save for them, as much as we can.'

'Oh, all right, all right. If you insist.' She slowly gets up and clambers out of her box.

We pad down to the galley and look around. I can't see any rats, but I can smell them.

'OK, any food you see, any bread, anything. Get what you can and we'll make another trail. Then we'll go to the stores and get more. Biscuits, anything. We'll have to use a little bit of food in order to save lots of food. We'll make a trail right up to the stern.'

Peggy is sniffing around. It isn't long before she finds some bread. It looks a bit green.

'Will this do?' she asks.

'Yes. Yes. Anything. And please don't eat any this time.' I feel like Kerans. Taking charge. Knowing what needs to be done.

We get the bread and find some more. We break it up with our paws and our teeth, as small as we can. We carry it all in our mouths and take it up near the stern. We make a trail of food in the small space between the box and the side of the ship before going back to the galley and looking for more food. We find some biscuits and some rice.

'Bite the biscuits, Peggy. Make them small. But no eating.'

'OK,' she grumbles. And she bites them and then presses her paw on them to make them even smaller. I collect some of the rice – ugh, it tastes horrible — and take that up too. We've made a trail and a nice pile of food on the stern. As we add to it, the pile gets bigger and the trail gets longer.

'Like Hamsel and Petal,' I smile at Peggy.

She gives me a funny look.

'I suppose we have to hide and wait again, like last time?' Peggy asks.

'Yes. And no falling asleep like before either.'

'Oh, don't you worry about that. I feel quite perky now, don't you know?' She nudges me. I wish her belly would swing like it used to. We hide and we wait.

I look at Peggy. She has her eyes open. That's good.

'What are you doing?' I ask her.

'What do you mean, what am I doing?' she answers. 'I'm thinking. I know I said I'm a doer and you're a thinker, but I seem to be doing a lot more of that these days.'

'What are you thinking about?' I ask her. I wonder what dog pictures are like.

'Oh, you know,' she replies. 'Stuff.' And she lets out a little parp.

'Sshh. Don't do that. You might scare the rats away. Or me.'

'Hmm. I don't think I could scare you away now, Simon. Brave little cat.'

A cat! So that's what I am! Not a me, but a cat.

We fall quiet. We wait. Both with our eyes open. My ears are back and listening. Peggy's ears are down. Both our noses are twitching.

And then... Squeak, squeak. Patter, patter. My fur stands on end and my claws stretch out. My nose twitches. I can smell them. Peggy goes to growl, but I make her shush.

I peep out and I can see them. I can see them coming. Rats and rats, following the trail, their pink feet and noses and their long tails. Running rats, eating all the food. *Our* food. I don't know how many there are, but there are lots of them. Some of them are up on the stern now, eating from the pile of biscuits and bread, rice and... other things. At the back I can see a big rat. The biggest of them all. Mao Tse Tung. It's him! He's sniffling and moving quite slowly, but he's coming towards us all the same.

I shrink back a little, but still watch them as they pass. More and more of them are running up to the stern. Mao Tse Tung scampers past me. I wait and I think of numbers in my head. Six, seven, eight, nine and another nine and another one. Right that will do. Goooo!

I jump out of my hiding place, spring forward and leap up to the stern. Ow! My back, my back legs, but I don't care. All we have is now. Peggy's right behind me. I get to the stern. The rats are all chomping away. Some of them don't even see me. I stretch my claws out, jump and... I grab one. I bite its back. It doesn't taste very nice, but I don't care. I keep on biting and clawing it until it stops moving; until finally it's dead.

Peggy's lying next to the bag, blocking the way. The rats can't get past her and they're too scared to try and run next to her and over the bag. They run round and round in circles. I grab another one and bite! Hard. And another and another. I catch another with my claws, bite it and add it to the slowly growing pile of dead ones. One rat, two rats, three rats, four.

My claws feel sharp, my eyes feel sharp. I feel... alive! I bite another rat and throw it onto the pile. They don't know where to run or what to do. Even Peggy catches one with her paw. I take it from her and do what I need to do.

I spy a shape standing behind Peggy. It's George. He must have heard the sound of rats squeaking and come out to see what's happening. He stands back, hiding in the shadows. I look down and see another rat running past me. Grab. Claw. Bite. Throw.

If Chairman and the Commies can attack us for no reason, then I can attack these rats for one huge, big, good reason. No more eating our food. No more nibbling on the sailors. I bite the back of another one and drag it over and… down into the water you go. Bat! With my paw. I catch another one and drop it over the side of the ship. I see Mao Tse Tung edging back, back but there's nowhere for him to go.

'Wait. Wait!' he hisses.

'I've waited long enough,' I meow right back at him. Oh, I like that. I reach forward, grab him, and bite the back of his neck and drag him across the stern. My, he's heavy. I bite and I bite. He's scrabbling under my claws, but I don't let go. I bite and he tries to scratch me. I bite and claw him again. Still he doesn't stop moving. Finally, with one extra hard bite, I feel my sharp teeth sink into his horrible neck. I know that, to be a cat, you have to act like a cat.

This is what I'm on this ship for. To face my fears, not to hide from them. I have him by the back of his neck and don't let go. With one last stretch of his pink feet, he goes limp. And stops moving. I let him go. He lies still in front of me. Stopped. Mao Tse Tung is dead!

I look up and hear George shout, 'Well done, Simon! You're a hero!'

Peggy wuffs her wuffiest wuff. 'You've done it!' she cries. 'Really done it this time. Wuff! Wuff! Wuff!'

I puff my chest out and stare at the lifeless body of Mao Tse Tung, the enemy of this ship. I bite into his neck again and half walk, half drag him off the stern, along the deck and up, up, up to the bridge. My back hurts, but I keep walking, keep dragging. There's a trail of red behind me. I reach the bridge, walk right up to Kerans and drop it at his feet.

He looks at the dead rat, looks at me and breaks out into a huge smile.

'I'll consider that a lucky charm. Well done, sailor.'

30/ A good plan

I'm in the mess deck feeling very pleased with myself. McCunnell's in here too. He gives me a smile and a stroke. George notices and whispers to me, 'Blimey, Simon, what's happened to him?'

Kerans comes in, sees me and winks before turning all serious and coughing.

'A typhoon's just passing China,' he tells them, 'So the banks of the Yangtze will be flooded. That means the Commies won't be there and the lookouts at Woosung forts won't be watching.'

All the sailors are staring at Kerans now.

'The moon sets at eleven this evening, that's when we'll have the best darkness.'

'Darkness for what, sir?' asks Atkins.

'So we can make a run for it.'

Some of the sailors gasp.

'HMS Concord is going to meet us at Woosung. Now, there's lots of work to be done in the next couple of hours and it's going to be hard. I know there's one fine sailor on here who's been doing some great work and I want you all to be just like him.'

George whispers to me. 'He means you, you know. You've made us happy with everything you've done.'

Me? What have I done apart from letting myself be stroked and… doing my job?

Kerans continues. 'I want sheets all around the ship. We'll disguise her as a ferry. That'll confuse them if we don't look like a war ship. And, when we set off, we'll use black smoke to confuse them even more.'

'Aye, sir,' Atkins says. 'Anything else?'

'Yes. I want you, you and you to fetch some hammocks and sheets and rub soft soap all over them,' and he points at three sailors.

'Why do you want us to do that?' Gurns asks. 'We don't have much soap left.'

'Just use everything we have,' Kerans snaps. 'Plenty of time for washing after we've made it through. We'll wrap them round the cable so, when it's time to slip anchor, she'll be a lot quieter. Right. Get to work everybody. We leave in a few hours. And in one hundred and forty miles — freedom.'

This all sounds exciting. It sounds as if we might be finally making our escape. Another adventure. I hope it's better than the one I'm in, because all this waiting and all this bad has just gone on for too, too long. I go to find Peggy.

She's in her box with her monkey, not sleeping, just staring.

'Kerans said we're going to run for it.'

Peggy's head lifts right up when she hears that.

'Oh good, because, you know, I really don't want to be here anymore. I hate it.'

Slowly, she climbs out and we head out on deck. It's cooler out here and the ship's lit up by the moon. I can see sailors everywhere, putting whatever they can over the side of the ship. No more flags, just dark, dark sheets.

'What are they doing?' Peggy asks.

'Hiding the ship,' I tell her.

'But I can still see it,' she says, puzzled.

'Just wait. You'll see,' and we sit down to watch the sailors preparing for whatever's about to happen next.

'No falling asleep,' I prod her.

'Fat chance of that,' she answers.

We lie on the deck, we watch and we wait. Kerans keeps walking past us, looking up at the sky and at something round his arm. Finally, he calls out to three sailors. 'Slip anchor.'

We stand up and run down to the huge chain. It's all wrapped up in hammocks and sheets. Slowly, it starts to move, but it doesn't make the noise it usually does. Whatever Kerans wanted the sailors to do must have worked because he's smiling and nodding on the bridge beside Hett. Then his face changes as he sees a brightly lit ship passing us on the river.

'Is that a ferry?' he cries. 'All right, let's wait for it to pass. We can go behind it. Might give us some extra cover.'

We watch and wait for the other ship to pass. Just as it gets quite small I hear Kerans shout an order again. 'OK, we need to do it now!'

Slowly, very, very slowly, our ship starts to move. I look up at some of the sailors who are standing around. Apart from the sound of the engine, it's very quiet. Nobody's speaking. The night sky is black; the ship is black; I'm black and white. I hope the Commies don't spot me. I duck down behind Peggy. I'm shaking.

'Come on, come on,' I hear someone mutter quietly.

I can see the ferry ahead of us, its lights blinking.

Just as I stop shaking and start to breathe properly, I hear a bang come from the land on the port side. Oh no! I see the faces of the sailors fall.

Peggy whimpers and I hear and smell what she does next.

'What shall we do? Where shall we go?' Suddenly, it gets darker. The ferry in front of us has put all its lights out. Bang! Bang! It's all dark, but I can't really see very far because of the smoke. I'm scared now. *Really* scared. And so are the sailors around me. We're not going to make it.

I feel the ship move faster before I hear someone shout, 'The ship! It's been hit!' But they don't mean us. They mean the one in front that we're sailing closer to. There's fire coming from it. They've hit the wrong ship!

31/ Escape

There's another bang. I hear something whizz past right in front of the bow and splash into the water. Quick! Quick! Come on! We get closer to the ferry. There are even more flames coming from it now. I feel sorry for the humans on there, but glad it's not us. Good and bad.

Bang! Our ship shakes. I think the bow's been hit. Come on! We sail right past the burning ferry. The land's on the other side of it. If the Commies fire again they'll just hit that one and not us. Keep going!

We pass right by it and sail on down the river. The banging stops.

'Quick,' I say to Peggy. 'Let's get below deck while we can.' We both move as fast as we can, running through the black smoke. Down in the mess deck it's very hot and smelly. I can hear a sound. It must be coming through the magic radio, but I'm too scared to wiggle my bottom. The sailors look scared too.

We wait and listen and wait.

Bang! Bang! Bang!

George picks me up and holds me very tight. I don't know who's shaking more, me or him.

Still the noises come. It sounds like it's from both sides now. Bang! Bang! Please don't let us be hit. No more. Please.

Peggy starts to cry and moves closer to Atkins. He rubs her head and gives her half a biscuit, but she doesn't even want it. 'You're getting too old for this, aren't you old girl?' he comforts her.

Bang!

There's a huge clang from outside. They must have hit us! We're not going to make it.

But we don't stop. We keep moving. Another bang, but no clanging sound. Then, the banging gets quieter. We must have got through. All the men breathe out. I wiggle and George sets me down.

I walk over to Peggy. We nuzzle each other before I slowly walk in between the sailors' legs, letting them stroke me if they want to.

'Seventy up.'

I don't know what that means but it's a big number. I want to go outside, to see if it's safe. Should I do it? If I count and count in my head and there are no bangs then, yes, I will do it. I will be brave. I think of all the numbers I know, small ones and then big ones. I don't get to seventy but I get to twenteen. I tell Peggy. 'I'm going to go out on deck.'

'Don't do it, Simon. Are you mad? Don't go.'

But I trot out and up the stairs. It's dark and smoky, but there are no bangs. I'm scared. I want to be brave. I think of Chairman. I think of JoJo. I run as fast as I can up to the bridge. Just as I get there, I hear the bangs again, coming from both sides of the ship.

'Increase speed,' Kerans shouts.

Faster! Faster! We're sailing through a very narrow bit of the river. That must mean we're even closer to the Commies. Bang! Bang! Come on! We move forward.

I wish I wasn't here. I wish JoJo was here. We keep going. Sometimes I think I hear bangs when there aren't any. Sometimes I hear bangs when there are. Each time I think of magic, of JoJo, of Uboat or Lilette.

Hett's face changes. 'We've reached one hundred up.'

I'm sure I can hear the sailors shouting. Is this good or bad? We haven't been hit, so I think it's good. I breathe out again.

Through the smoke, I see... I don't know what they are. Huge, bright lights moving up and down on the dark water, like lots of suns peeping out from behind clouds.

'There are lights looking for us. Careful now.'

What will happen if they see the ship? I watch the lights on the water. They're moving fast, but they don't touch the ship. We move through them. Still they don't touch us. There are no bangs, but it's all still very, very scary.

And then. And then...

'Look ahead!' Kerans shouts. 'I think I see the Concord. I think we've made it!'

My ears prick. My whiskers quiver. Does that mean there won't be any more bangs? Have we done it? Have we escaped?

I stare up at Kerans and Hett. They shake hands, they're both happy. I'm surrounded by happy. Kerans has a big, big smile on his face. He looks happier than I've ever seen him before. The Concord flashes at us and Kerans and Hett both laugh.

Kerans puts his mouth over the thing again. 'Concord in sight and signal has been received. Please send a signal in return: 'Never, never, has a ship been more welcome.''

I run as fast as I can out of the bridge, down the starboard, no — port — oh, it doesn't matter — side and head back to the mess deck. I'm moving so fast I can feel my back hurting again, but I don't care because I'm not dead. I even spy a rat on my way back and pounce on it. Bite! Take that.

When I reach the mess deck, all the sailors are jumping up and down or moving around, holding each other, just like the men with the shiny buttons and the women who smell nice back in the place where I'm from. The sailors are all cheering, so loud it makes my ears hurt. Some of them even have wet eyes although I don't know why because this is all happy, not sad. Peggy's running around in a circle, trying to catch her wagging tail.

George picks me up and spins me round. I'm flying, flying, spinning, spinning. 'Oh, you little beauty.' He even kisses me on the nose.

Some of us go out on deck and see the Concord and the sailors on it waving at us. I wish I could wave back, but then George lifts up my port paw and does it for me.

Kerans comes down from the bridge to join us and is met with cries of, 'Well done, sir!'

'And well done to you all,' he replies. 'And you too,' and he rubs my head, but doesn't kiss me on my nose. 'I've signalled the Commander in Chief to say we are OK. Even the King has said well done! God save the King.''

'God save the King!' the sailors all call back. 'And God save you,' says George to me, quietly.

Crew: The four in the middle of the front row are, left to right:
Hett, Kerans, Strain, Fearnley
Photo from Lieutenant Commander Stewart Hett

32/ Winning medals

It's Wednesday, the 3rd of August 1949. We had been stuck for over one hundred days. Even though I don't know what this means I know it must be important because George said so.

We're sailing into Hong Kong, the place where I... used to be from. There are three ships sailing in front of us, but they are all our friends.

As we get close, I see lots of humans standing, looking up at us. When they see us, all of them cheer and wave. They have things round their necks and, when they hold them up to their faces, flashes of sunshine come out of them. It feels as if they are trying to blind me. I keep turning away so they see my bottom, not my face.

George points down to them from where we are standing at the bow, with me tucked under his arms. 'That's for you.'

Why, what have I done? Maybe they've heard about the rats?

'As of now, you're all off for twenty-four hours,' Kerans tells the sailors and they cheer, as loud as the humans down on the dock. Some of them throw their hats in the air.

'The commander's arranged a party for us all. Free drinks,' Kerans tells them.

Laughter and smiles. They walk, no, they *run* down the tongue.

'What d'you think, Simon?' George asks me. 'D'you want to go to a party?'

I don't know what one is, but I like the sound of it and I want to get away from the flashes of sunshine and all the noise. Maybe Peggy should come too? Where is she? Oh there she is, right at the front, her monkey in her mouth, wagging her tail, excited to get off.

We walk up some stairs into a big building. It smells fresh and clean. Everything's big. Huge lights hang down from the ceiling.

We go through a doorway and humans hit their hands together when they see Kerans, George, me and the other sailors. There are lots of chairs and tables around with the yummiest looking food on them. I wonder if they have any Whiskers, though I hope they don't have any brown drink.

We sit round a table. I'm on George's knee. He passes me a plate with fish on and other things. I sniff round the plate, eating what I like, leaving what I don't. Peggy is underneath the table. I can hear her. Not making her usual noise though, she is just gobbling down lots and lots of food.

The humans all seem to know which silver shiny things to use and when to use them. I wonder whether I would prefer to use the shiny things to eat my food or if I'm happy as I am. I look at my claws and think about what I've been doing with them. I lick the plate with my tongue.

I'm happy I'm me, but there's a bit of me that wants to fly like a bird and, when I look at those humans over there, I realise there's a bit of me that would quite like to be a human too, just for a short while, so I could do what they're doing now.

Kerans walks through the doorway and everybody goes quiet.

'Ladies and Gentlemen. As I'm sure you all know, the crew of the Amethyst and I have been through the most horrible one hundred or so days. If it wasn't for the strength, courage and bravery of our men, well, I don't think we would have made it.'

There's lots of nodding and muttering from everyone.

'However,' Kerans continues. 'It's also thanks to two very special friends on board our ship that we all got through. Simon here... ' I look up, '...has been clever at keeping the spirits of our men up and the population of our rats down while on board. And Peggy—'

I hear a knock under the table. She must have bumped her head.

'Where is Peggy?' Kerans looks around. Slowly, she comes out from under the table, looking guilty. 'Peggy here has also been a great addition to the crew. If it wasn't for these two, well, I don't know what it would have been like. Seacat Simon here... '

That's me.

'...has been awarded the Dickin Medal, an important animals' award for bravery. I don't have the medal yet but, in honour of Simon and everything he has done, and not forgetting Peggy of course, I want you all to stand now and raise your glasses to these two great sailors, while I pin a ribbon on them both.'

Everybody in the room stands, looks at me and hits and hits their hands together. Over and over again. Kerans leans forward and tries to attack me with the ribbon in his hand. Uh oh, I must really be in trouble. Quickly, I jump off the table and hide under it so I don't get attacked. Peggy joins me.

George sticks his head under the table, reaches down, grabs me and plonks me back on the table.

Kerans hands a ribbon to him which he quickly wraps round my neck before bending down to wrap one around Peggy's neck too.

I don't like it. It itches. I try to bite it off. Peggy looks up at me, her tail wagging. 'Well? What do you think?' she asks. 'Do I look dashing?'

She looks like Peggy with a ribbon. I ask her what's going on.

'You've been awarded a medal, Simon. For being so brave.'

Am I brave now? Am I really? Finally. But I don't really want a medal. I don't even know what one is. I just want to be with my friends.

33/ Losing a friend

I don't know how long we stay in the nice place, but when I leave with George, Peggy and Atkins holding Peggy's toy monkey, it's getting darker and cooler.

Through the narrow alleys and streets, we wander in and out of shops. George buys a yellow, curved thing and Atkins buys a hairy, round, brown thing. It's nice to be back in a place again where I remember a lot of the smells. It smells of... home. We turn down another alleyway. Peggy is in front until we reach a narrow street I half recognise.

A shop — ah yes — I know where we are now and Peggy trots right in and sits down on the floor. The owner looks at Atkins and at me in George's arms, then she spies Peggy and she smiles. 'Oh, back again! My, what happen you? You all thin. You need good feed.'

Peggy's tail goes thump, thump, thump on the floor. Atkins and George look around the shop. They keep holding things up and laughing.

'Peggy! Come on! We need to go now,' I tell her, when they're ready to leave.

She looks at me but she doesn't move.

'I'm sorry, Simon, I'm not coming back with you.'

'What d'you mean?' I mew. 'Not coming back? We belong on the ship. We live there.'

'I'm very sorry, Simon. Really I am. I've been doing an awful lot of thinking and not much doing recently. Like you.'

'You see, I'm old now, Simon. And after all we've been through, well, I think it's time I moved on.' She looks very sad.

'But we live on there!' I cry.

'No, Simon. *You* live on there. You have a job to do. All I do now is get in everybody's way and wait under the tables for them to drop their food. I don't really do anything. Not anymore.'

'But you're my friend.' I bat her nose with my paw, but she just lies down. 'You're my best friend. You make me happy.'

'No, Simon, you make you happy. I'm just a silly old fuss bag.'

This can't be happening. This can't be right. Not Peggy. Peggy who first looked after me when George brought me on board. Peggy who showed me around the ship and introduced me to Pauloni. Peggy with her licks and her smells and her monkey.

'Here, Peggy,' Atkins calls to her. 'Here girl, come on.'

But she doesn't move. She just lies there.

'I'm going to stay here, Simon,' she says quietly. 'The owner has already gone to get me a nice bowl of something scrumptious.'

'No, Peggy! You can't! You can't!' I cry again. But I can tell by the look in her eyes that she won't budge. She won't be coming back with us. George and Atkins call her and call her, but she won't stand up and come over. The owner walks over from the back of the shop and places a red bowl full of food right in front of Peggy. She nudges her monkey out of the way and tucks right in.

'Stubborn as a mule, that one,' Atkins says to George.

She's not a mule. She's a dog. A fat, silly, smelly, lovely, funny dog. My dog.

'Looks like you've got a lodger,' George says to the owner, laughing.

'She been coming here for long time,' the owner replies. 'I always say she welcome to stay.'

'Maybe she's getting a little too old for the ship now,' Atkins says as he watches Peggy tucking in. He turns to the owner. 'Well, if you're sure...?'

George looks down at Peggy too. 'And it seems like she's already made her mind up.'

The owner smiles at George and Atkins. 'She be happy here with me. I look after her good.'

George and Atkins glance at each other, then both slowly bend down to give Peggy a farewell ruffle. I see that there's wet in George's eyes again.

'Come on,' he says quietly, 'Let's go.' They walk out of the shop, but I run right over to Peggy.

'You're really going to stay here, then?' I ask her.

'Mmm, hurr,' she munches. And then looks up. 'It's for the best Simon, really it is. You're all going to be sailing home and I honestly don't think I'll even be able to make it. I think here will be simply a splendid place to spend my golden years.'

I am sad, sad, sad. This isn't right. I try one last try. 'But now is all we have.' I mew again.

'Yes,' she answers slowly. 'And I don't have many 'nows' left. So, everything we had up to now is what we have too. Don't forget that.'

She puts her face up to mine and rubs my nose with hers.

'Bye, Simon, it's been most awfully good fun spending time with you but, you know what they say, all good things must come to an end.' She gives me a lick.

Why must they?

I give her a nuzzle. One last nuzzle.

I turn and walk out of the shop to join George and Atkins.

'Simon,' I hear Peggy call. I turn around in the doorway and look back at her.

'Remember — you're magic.'

George picks me up. He must know I'm feeling very sad because he squeezes me extra tight. Slowly we walk back to the ship. What am I going to do without Peggy? Maybe I could have stayed there with her? But I feel like I belong more on the ship now than I do here, where I am from. Was from. Now I need to carry on being brave, but in a different way.

George rubs my head. I look around at what I used to know and, when we reach the ship, at what I know now. We walk up the tongue. It makes me think of Peggy and her licky tongue. Up and up we go, back onto the deck, back to the place where I'm now from. I turn around to have one last look at the port. The port where I used to run and play, before all this. As I look, I'm sure I can see, running in and out between some baskets, a beautiful white cat.

145

34/ Home for some

It's grey and cold and I don't know how I feel. We're sailing into Plymouth in England. England is home to the sailors on here. The place where they're from. I know it isn't my home, but I suppose it will be now. I miss Peggy though.

We stopped at lots of places on the way here and were greeted by cheering crowds and happy and smiling faces. It's good to know that not all humans want to see other humans dead and gone. And everywhere we went there were flashes of sunshine by humans coming on board and pointing clicky things at me. I didn't like it; I don't know why anyone would like it. But everyone seems to want to see me and people everywhere keep saying I'm a hero, so I suppose they must like me, even if I don't like their click, clicks.

We've been sailing for ten thousand miles, George says. That's the biggest number I've ever heard of. A lot more than twenteen. There are more humans waiting for us here in Plymouth than anywhere else we've stopped. Lots of them all lined up, some of them looking very smart, but all of them shouting, calling, waving.

George is smiling too. 'This is home,' he says to me. 'I hope you like it.' He lifts up my front port paw to wave at the humans. I'm glad we're getting off, but I'm so tired. I just want to be with people I love.

The ship docks with one last blast of the horn and I'm nearly made deaf by the roar of the crowd. The big tongue is laid down. Not long now until I can get off. I wait for George to pick me up, but it doesn't happen. Instead, two very important looking men come on board and shake hands with Kerans.

A man walks up to me. He's carrying a huge bag. 'Seacat Simon,' and he stands up straight, bangs his feet together and puts his starboard hand to his head. 'For you.' He opens the bag and pulls out lots and lots and lots of… I don't know what they are. Papers with squiggly lines on; tins of I-don't-know-what; small cloth creatures that look a bit like Peggy's smelly old monkey. What am I supposed to do with these?

'The whole world loves you,' he says.

I think I should purr, but I don't. I just think of those who love me, but who aren't here.

I look round for George, but I can't see him. More and more sailors are getting off the ship; it's getting emptier and emptier. From nowhere, the man who showed me all of the I-don't-know-whats hands me a saucer of something white to drink. I give it a lick. It's... OK.

And then, I look up... and no one's left on the ship except me. I'm happy and I'm sad. What shall I do now? Shall I look for rats? Are there any rats left to catch? I stretch out and lie on the deck. Ouch! My back. I forget it still hurts sometimes. This is the first time I've been on my own. First there was JoJo and then there was Peggy, George and the sailors. I know they'll come back though, so I still feel a little bit more good than bad.

35/ Not flying, but moving

After all the sailors had gone, I was looking forward to giving myself a nice old lick and clean. I was just about to settle down when the man who gave me the saucer with something white in crept up behind me, scooped me up and put me in a box. He spun me round a bit too fast and it made me feel dizzy. I didn't feel like I was flying; I just felt as if I was caught.

Then he put me and the box in a car. The car coughed and now we are rattling along — bump, bump, bump. I've never been in a car before. I don't like it! It makes this box move around and, every time it bumps, I bump my head on the top of the box.

I don't know where we're going. I suppose we must be going to George's. I feel like I did when I sicked up some pilchard back on the ship.

After a long, long time, the car stops. Phew. George really must live very far away from where the ship docked. Why didn't the ship just dock nearer to where he lived?

The car door opens and I'm slid along, and then up and out of the car. Don't spin me round too fast! I hear the crunch of the man's footsteps as we walk up to George's big, big house with lots of lights on.

The man opens a door and we walk in. It's very bright. It hurts my eyes a little. I see some chairs all lined up and pictures of cats on the walls, but no George. Oh well, he's probably making me some lovely food. The man lifts me up and places me on what looks like a counter. It smells all clean in here. I can see a girl and another human. The girl looks at me and smiles. She has black hair and red lips. She puts her fingers through the bars.

'Welcome, Simon. I've heard so much about you. Read about you too.'

George must have told her all about me. I wonder if this is George's girl-brother. I peer out at the pictures of the cats on the walls. Who are they? Why didn't George tell me about them? The clean smell and the bright light and all the cats looking at me make me feel lightheaded.

The girl smiles at me. 'My name's Molly. We just need to check you over and then you can go and rest. Haven't you had a long journey?'

Yes. Ten thousand miles, George said. And then all the way from the ship to George's home. I'm tired. But I can't sleep because Molly and the man prod me and turn me over and pull my ears and lift up my tail. They make lots of squiggly lines on paper and stick something up my bottom and sting me in my side like those yellow and black buzzy things. If this is a hello, I wish they'd say goodbye!

Molly takes me into a room. A room that George still isn't in. She places a bowl of the white stuff for me to drink and fetches a tin. I recognise the picture on it straight away. How did she know? Maybe George told her how much I like it, so she got some for me specially. I like Molly.

After I've eaten, she takes me outside to a little garden.

'OK, here you can come and play two times a day, but you can't play with any of the other cats yet.'

So there are other cats here? That's nice. I wonder how many there are. So that means I'll have lots of new friends as well as George. How odd I'm not allowed to play with them yet. Maybe they've heard what I did to the rats and are scared of me. It might not feel so good at the moment, but I know it will soon all be good, good, good. I run around and sniff. Yes, I can smell other cats. I can't smell George though.

I close my eyes. I want to hear George say, 'Hello, Simon,' before I open them. But he doesn't say hello. Nobody says hello. Instead, I hear a clang and feel my paws land on something hard. I open my eyes and turn around quickly. More bars, with Molly's face peering at me from the other side of them.

'There's a good cat.'

The bars clang shut. I am trapped and alone again.

36/ Time to go

When can I leave here? When will I stop hurting?

'There, there.' Molly is stroking me. 'Can't you have just a little bit more? Just a little bit?'

But I don't want to eat any more Whiskers. This isn't home. This is a place called quarantine and I don't want to *be* here. George has seen me a few times. He says all animals have to come here when they have been travelling in case we are poorly. That's why I can't talk to the other cats yet either.

He said he and my other friends went to something called a gala dinner in a place called the Dorchester Hotel. It means they ate lots of food. I wish I'd been there.

And they met the Lord Mayor one day too. I know who he is. Peggy told me about him. He's called Dick Whittington and he had a cat who was very good at catching rats. Like me. Like I used to be.

George says I have to stay here for six months and then I can go and live with Kerans. I don't know why I'm here. If this is what happens after you've been brave then I wish I hadn't been brave. I was happier when I was scared all the time and I had George to look after me.

I know I'm good, I know I haven't been bad, so why do I have to be here? Maybe it's just the unlucky part of me after I've been so lucky for such a long time. So if lucky means good and unlucky means bad, then maybe there really is some bad in me after all?

Kerans says Hett is now Cat Officer as so many people know about me. Whenever he comes to see me he brings a bag and shows me presents that humans have sent me from around the world. If I really were magic I would make it so that, when he opens the bag, Peggy would come out! Or JoJo of course. Kerans tells me how the world loves me, but I don't feel loved. I just feel left and alone.

I do like Molly though. She feeds me and strokes me and she smells of outside. We go out into the garden too. I wish I could fly

away from here until I found the sea, then I would look for the
Amethyst and land on it.

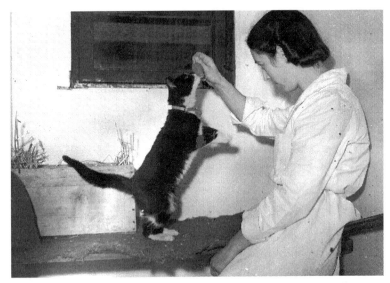

Simon in quarantine with one of the kennel maids
Photo from the PDSA

I would find Peggy in her box with her monkey and we'd run
and hide and play.

I hear the ring of the doorbell. That means someone's here.
Molly stands up.

'I'll just go and see who it is,' and she steps out of the little
room.

'Simon,' she calls when she steps back in. 'Visitor for you.'

I look up and see George. I want to jump up, but all I can do is
slowly stand.

'Hey, Simon.'

I purr at him. Molly is standing next to George.

'How does it feel to be the world's most famous cat?' George
smiles at me.

It feels lonely.

'I've got some good news for you,' George smiles at me.

Good news at last! What is it?

'They've arranged a ceremony for you in two weeks' time. You're so famous that Maria Dickin will be there to award you your medal herself. *And* the Lord Mayor.'

The Lord Mayor? How exciting! I hope he brings his cat. I might have someone to talk to, not like these other cats in here with me.

'Oh, I've brought you this as well. I found it earlier.' George reaches into his pocket and pulls something out. It's the die! I sniff it. I sniff and sniff. I'm sure I can smell Peggy on it.

'I have to go now. But only two weeks. Two weeks, Simon, until your big day. But I'll be back before then.'

And then he is gone.

Later on, after Molly has tried to feed me some more Whiskers, I'm out in the garden. It's night time. I look up at the moon. I wonder if it's the same as the one I saw many times on the ship.

I'm just about to go back inside to play with my die and give it another sniff when I suddenly feel all funny.

Soon I can feel soft hands pick me up, up. Soft hands which must be Molly's.

'Hang on, Simon, the vet's on his way. You just hold on, there's a brave chap.'

A vet? A Hett?

'Now Simon, how's the bravest cat in quarantine doing? Oh dear, you don't look your usual self at all. Let's see what we can do about that, shall we?' the man asks.

I'm hot and cold. I'm happy and sad. I'm awake. I'm sleeping. I'm scared. I'm brave. I'm alone.

'Right, Simon, I'm going to leave Molly to look after you for a while. You rest, old chap, and show us all why they're giving you that medal, all right?' I hear the vet say.

'You're such a brave cat,' whispers Molly, crying. 'How about some water, Simon? Come on, just a little, you're very hot.'

In my head I see Uboat and we're playing near the cool, blue sea. No, it's Lilette. Oh, I'm so mixed up. I feel as if I can smell her and see white, the white of Lilette's fur. She's smiling and I'm being stroked and brushed.

No, I'm wrong. Maybe it's Peggy. I should have known that lovely, wobbly body anywhere. I'm surprised I didn't smell her or hear her parp! She can't really be here. Maybe it's in my head I'm chasing her.

'You're a dog,' I call after her.

'And you are a wonderfully brave cat.'

Where's Peggy? Where's Lilette? Where's Uboat gone? They must be somewhere. They *must* be. I've seen them. I know what's pretend and what's real and this is real. It is. I think. Oh, I don't know anymore. My head is all muddled.

'Titch?'

No! It can't be, can it? Yes, yes it is. It's JoJo! He's walking towards me. I think.

'Oh, JoJo! JoJo! I've missed you so much. I have so many stories... '

'I know you do. You're a wonderful little brother to have. You've done so many things... '

He looks the same, he smells the same, he *is* the same. Where has he been? It's so lovely to have him back.

Oh! JoJo? JoJo? Where's he gone? I look around, but I can't see him.

'Keep fighting, Simon. Show us all that brave little you that everyone's talking about,' Molly says. I hear her crying. It makes me sad. Please don't cry, Moggy.

I feel scared again. And then... A shape. Who is it? What is it? The shape gets closer and closer. It's black and it's white. Then I see who it is. I know who it is. Yes, I would rather be here. I'm not scared. I'm not alone. It's mother! My mother!

She gives me a lovely lick and cuddles right, right up to me. She's lovely and warm and soft.

'Come now.' She sounds as if she's very far away. 'I'm here. Nothing can harm you now.'

154

'Oh mother, mother. I wish you'd never left me.'

'I never left you, you silly boy.'

'You did! You left me. Then JoJo left me. I hid, I was so scared. I was shaking.'

'Not all of you was shaking. Your tail was sticking out.'

'You mean...?'

'Yes,' she nuzzles me. 'I was always there. Helping you. Making sure you knew what to do so someone would find you.'

She cuddles me. I'm warm. I'm safe.

'Will it...? Will everything...? Is it all going to be OK, mother?'

'Yes. Yes, you're with me now. Come rest against me, feel my fur against yours.'

I'm purring now. So happy! I feel no pain. Just my mother beside me, her warm body around mine, her tail wrapped around me. I hear nothing but her soft voice.

'We've to go now.' She cuddles me. I know where I'm from and where I'm not from. I know I have to go away. My mother's comforting me, soothing me. I hear her, far away, yet closer.

'It's time.'

My eyes are open. The sky is bright. I wish I could fly away. I close my eyes. I can smell her, feel her, hear her. I'm not in quarantine anymore. I'm here. Where I belong. I'm surrounded by my mother, by her warmth, by her breath. I think I *really* know what love is now.

My mother's face right up, up, close, close to mine. I look into her soft, round eyes and her whiskers touch mine.

'Come on now, my beautiful boy,' she smiles at me. For the last time. For the first time.

'Let's go home.'

I feel so, so happy. So loved. So safe.

37/ Afterwards

Seaman McCunnell here. Simon's sadly no longer with us. George was the last of the Amethyst sailors to see him. He'd visited Simon the night before to tell him the news about the award ceremony. A vet was sent for as Simon was very poorly, but he couldn't fix him. He thought Simon's heart was just too weak after all he went through when the ship was hit.

I'm so glad George found Simon. Sorry — Seacat Simon. I know I didn't much like him when he first appeared, but he really cheered me and the others up. And as for the rats! I don't know what we would have done without Simon, specially when he killed Mao Tse Tung. Huge thing, it was. We all had a go at catching him, but it was Simon who finally did.

We were all really sad when George told us about Simon not being around anymore. But he was such a brave cat on the ship that he was awarded several medals. Kerans and his wife went to collect them and keep them safe. We all went to watch that day too as Simon had been so special to us. It felt as if he was watching over us.

It's so sad Simon is no longer with us, but we have to be happy that we were lucky enough to know him and have him in our lives. I know my life was all the better for having Simon in it. I'm so glad I became friends with him before it was too late.

Simon was such a good little cat, always helping others. He was a great reminder of just how much good there can be in the world, no matter where you find it, or how small and furry it is.

We will never forget Simon and I hope you won't forget his story either.

Seaman McCunnell

157

Simon's PDSA Dickin Medal.
Photo from Eaton Film Company who bought it in 1993.

Message from Jacky Donovan

If you've enjoyed reading *Seacat Simon: The little cat who became a big hero* I would love it if you could ask your family to put a review on Amazon for you. It helps other people decide whether to buy the book.

Please ask them to join my mailing list so you are amongst the first to receive details of my next children's book.

Jacky Donovan

Level 1 quiz questions

How many of these questions can you answer correctly? The answers are in the next section, but no peeping until you have tried!

A. *Dark time.* What does Simon mean when he says this?
   a. Day time
   b. Night time
   c. Play time

B. *Like George, they're lying back and swinging in tiny beds hanging up.* What are the beds called that Simon is talking about?
   a. Bunk beds
   b. Sun beds
   c. Hammocks

C. *He is dressed in white, holding a drink and has fog coming out of his mouth.* What is the Captain doing?
   a. Smoking
   b. Singing
   c. Talking

D. *I bat my paw and can feel something. It makes a sound against the side of the jug. I twist my paw around and fish out the cold thing I can feel and hear, but cannot really see.* What has Simon found in the jug?
   a. Fish
   b. Fruit
   c. Ice cubes

E. *He's holding something in his hand and moving it around. Lots of marks appear on the paper as he moves his hand.* What is George doing?
   a. Reading a book

b. Writing

c. Using a magic wand

F. *I look back at him and his eyes are all wet.* Why are George's eyes wet?

    a. He is crying

    b. He is talking

    c. He is sleeping

G. *He also has a very big pair of long, round things that he puts up to his face and then looks around.* What is the Captain holding?

    a. A newspaper

    b. Binoculars

    c. His glasses

H. *As I look back up at the clothes, I can see some... I don't know what they are... swinging about. One of them pulls some washing down as it climbs down the walls, swinging and jumping. They look like tiny furry children, not quite human. I can hear noise, not quite talking.* What do you think Simon has seen?

    a. Monkeys

    b. Mice

    c. Birds

I. *Sometimes I almost feel as if we're as close as a brother and a girl-brother.* What word is Simon looking for when he says 'girl-brother'?

    a. Aunt

    b. Grandmother

    c. Sister

J. *He feels around, finds what looks like a little white flag in his pocket, dips it into the jug and dabs the Captain's face with it.* What word is Simon looking for when he says 'white flag'?

    a. Table cloth

    b. Hanky

  c. Newspaper

K. *'Attention!' and all the sailors stop eating, stand up straight away and hit the side of their head with their starboard hand.* What are the sailors doing here?

  a. Clapping

  b. Saluting

  c. Playing games

L. *George buys a yellow, curved thing and Atkins buys a hairy, round, brown thing.* What did George and Atkins buy?

  a. Banana and kiwi fruit

  b. Lemon and coconut

  c. Banana and coconut

Level 1 quiz answers

A. b
B. c
C. a
D. c
E. b
F. a
G. b
H. a
I. c
J. b
K. b
L. c

How many did you get right?

9 or more: Congratulations! You're a super Seacat Simon star.

Between 5 and 8: Well done! You're a great Seacat Simon fan.

Less than 5: Never mind. Why not have another try?

Level 2 quiz questions

A. *Whenever lovely sounds come from inside there are always men and women moving around close together and it makes me want to wiggle my bottom a little bit.* What is Simon talking about here?

    a. The people are dancing and he wants to join in

    b. The people are walking

    c. The people are watching television

B. *'Well, on here you need to be much more considerate where you go about doing your, er, business,'* she gives a little cough. *'Otherwise you get into the most awful trouble.'* What is Peggy talking to Simon about?

    a. Going to the toilet

    b. Going to eat

    c. Going to sleep

C. *'Ah, put a sock in it, Conway,'* George shouts over to him. *'I'll sock you in half a jiffy,'* Conway calls back. *Why are they talking about socks, Simon wonders.* What does the word 'sock' mean in each of these sentences?

    a. Put your socks on / I'll take my socks off / things you wear on your feet

    b. Be quiet / I'll hit you / things you wear on your feet

    c. Eat your socks / I'll throw my sock at you / things you wear on your feet

D. *His starboard pocket.* Which pocket does Simon mean? Do you know which is port and which is starboard?

    a. His left pocket. Port means right and starboard means left.

    b. His right pocket. Port means left and starboard means right.

E. *'Sunk more than one U-boat with this, I have.'* What is the U-boat the Captain is talking about? It certainly isn't Simon's friend Uboat!

    a. A submarine

    b. A house

    c. A car

F. What is the difference between Whiskas and whiskers?

    a. They are the same thing

    b. One is cat food and the other is the hairs on a cat's face

G. *'Hello,' she replies. 'I'm not sure I ever knew your name.' 'It's Simon,' I reply. I still feel a bit shy around her, especially when I tell her my name. Even Uboat gives me a funny look when I tell her.'* Why does Uboat give Simon a funny when Simon tells Lilette his name?

    a. He is always laughing at Simon

    b. He knows Simon was called Titch until he started to live on the ship

H. *It must be Peggy's smelly old sock toy monkey. I might not know what a monkey is, but by the look of this one I really hope I do one day because they look cute and lovely.* Why do you think Simon doesn't know he has seen monkeys before?

    a. Peggy's toy monkey looks cute and the monkeys Simon met were cruel so he doesn't realise they are all monkeys

    b. Simon has forgotten he had a horrible time with the monkeys who threw him around and scratched him

I. *They have things round their necks and, when they hold them up to their faces, flashes of sunshine come out of them.* What are the people using?

    a. Cigarettes

    b. Newspapers

    c. Cameras

J. *Humans hit their hands together when they see Kerans, George, me and the other sailors.* What are the people doing?

    a. Fighting

    b. Clapping

    c. Dancing

K. *And they met the Lord Mayor one day too. I know who he is. Peggy told me about him. He's called Dick Whittington and he had a cat who was very good at catching rats. Like me. Like I used to be.* Do you think the sailors really met Dick Whittington?

    a. No, the story of Dick Whittington took place hundreds of years before Simon was alive

    b. Yes, everyone who goes to London meets Dick Whittington

L. *'Oh mother, mother. I wish you'd never left me.'*

    'I never left you, you silly boy.'

    'You did! You left me. Then JoJo left me. I hid, I was so scared. I was shaking.'

    'Not all of you was shaking. Your tail was sticking out.'

    'You mean...?'

    'Yes,' she nuzzles me. 'I was always there. Helping you. Making sure someone would find you.'

How had Simon's mother helped him at the start of the story?

    a. She sang to him
    b. She helped him make his tail stick out so George would see him
    c. She gave him some food

Level 2 quiz answers

A. a
B. a
C. b
D. b
E. a
F. b
G. b
H. a
I. c
J. b
K. a
L. b

How many did you get right?

9 or more: Congratulations! You're a Seacat Simon superstar.

Between 5 and 8: Well done! You're a Seacat Simon expert.

Less than 5: Never mind. Why not have another try?

www.SimonShipsOut.com

Made in the USA
Middletown, DE
13 November 2021

52350060R00106